*Jim Asherman MD*

# The Next Prescription

also by Jimmie Ashcraft, M.D.

*Reflections of a Country Doctor*

# The Next Prescription

## More Reflections
## of a Country Doctor

by

Jimmie Ashcraft, M.D.

First published by Dog Ear Publishing
4010 W. 86th Street, Ste H
Indianapolis, IN 46268
www.dogearpublishing.net

ISBN: 978-145750-542-3

This book is printed on acid-free paper.

Printed in the United States of America

This book is dedicated to Kay,

the love of my life, my lifetime companion, and best friend,


and to our children,

Jennifer, Rebecca, and David,

the shining stars in our lives.

# Contents

# Foreword

## My Huckleberry Friend and Me

I have traveled around with Jim visiting about his first book *Reflections of a Country Doctor,* and folks have asked me what my life was like as a doctor's wife. I would often tell them that I didn't think it was much different from other spouses. As I'm thinking about it some 46 years later, I realize that I had to be pretty independent and flexible. After years of having phone calls interrupt suppers and our children's activities, I planned things expecting to be interrupted. His priorities (or perhaps those of his patients) came first, and we came second much of the time.

The demands on a physician's time are significant. If I hadn't worked for wonderful doctors during Jim's time in medical school, I might not have understood those demands. During the training years, doctors wore beeper or pagers, not cell phones or Blackberries. The constant ringing and interrupted announcements of "paging Dr. Somebody" played like elevator music through the hospital and clinic. During my work as a medical secretary, I observed the various temperaments of physicians. Most physicians were caring and even endearing individuals. Some, however, were the rear end of a donkey. I knew early on that we would meet both types in private practice and tried to select a community where we could interact with mostly caring individuals.

Since Jim's practice served all of Eastern Montana there were always demands on his time. If he was in town, he was on call and available. I arranged our family vacations to correspond with his medical meetings and educational sessions. We took extra days to enjoy new places and fun activities with our children.

Early on, physician spouses (then mostly women) were encouraged to learn about the AMA (American Medical Association) and its Auxiliary. The Auxiliary allowed me to see medical spouses involved with community health issues, legislative issues, and fund raising activities. Some of these women worked full time jobs and some did not. I found the opportunity in the Auxiliary (now called the AMA Alliance) to learn about medical and health issues facing medicine and our community. I was honored to serve as Montana State Alliance President as well as a Field Director for the AMA Alliance. As a state and national officer, I made wonderful memories and friendships at meetings held in windy Chicago.

In a small community most people thought I knew their medical problems, when in fact I did not. Jim would speak in generalities about issues or problems of the day, but he always kept patient's confidences. I tried hard not to become involved with small town gossip. Even though I was an office employee, I maintained the financial books at home and seldom worked in the office itself. Sometimes I overheard conversations about the medical staff or someone in particular. Some comments hurt personally like calling the fitness center "Ashcraft's Folly." That project, by the way, turned out to be a national one-of a-kind fitness facility and became a good marketing tool for recruiting staff for the hospital. Many people helped sustain the commitment Jim and I made in 1976 to see Sidney have a great medical facility.

Small towns provide a wonderful opportunity to volunteer. I was elected to the school board, started a volunteer program at the hospital, helped with fund raising for the law enforcement drug education program (DARE), coached softball and volleyball, lunched with "the committee" and played Bonko every month with a terrific group of ladies. We were fortunate to live in a community with a good school system and a community involved with its citizens' needs.

Why didn't I have an 8 to 5 job? Because I knew the demands required of my physician husband, and I didn't want someone else to raise our kids. I had various opportunities to use my teaching degree, though most were unpaid positions. Now that I'm retired, I wonder how my family or I would be different if I had chosen to work outside the home or if I needed a paying job. We would have matured differently, dreamed differently, or handled situations differently. For me, actively parenting our children was my calling in life.

Despite maintaining a busy home, I was involved with Jim's practice. Knowing when, where, why, what, and how the money flows is a good thing for all spouses to understand. On occasion, our income would dwindle when we received beef, lamb, eggs and gingerbread houses for payment. Fortunately, we had excellent personnel who kept the office working smoothly for us. Being a self-employed, solo practitioner presented unique financial challenges that most clinic or hospital employed physicians don't face today. We took our commitments to our employees seriously, and we were always the last to be paid.

On the home front, I was mostly in charge. The acre of yard and garden kept the kids and me busy mowing, weeding and irrigating when Jim would get called away. He sometimes left the field in his shorts and work boots to change into hospital scrubs just in time to catch a newborn baby. A woman in labor doesn't wait for the field work to be done. We very seldom waited supper for him and when the kids were very small they were usually in bed when he came home. I always knew that the people Jim worked with depended on him to answer their calls and respond quickly. The kids understood that as well. Our twenty acres in the country provided our mental health and physical therapy sessions.

Being a doctor's wife does come in handy when the kids need help. When our daughter Becky hit her forehead on the panic bar on the door at school one slick morning there was no wait time in the ER. We just brought her to the office. When son David broke his hand playing American Legion baseball one summer just ten days before he went off to college, Doctor dad took him to the hand surgeon in Billings so he wouldn't miss his first day of classes. The day our oldest daughter Jennifer delivered her twin girls, Doctor grandpa was scrubbed in for the c-section along side her family doc and obstetrician.

Medical marriage is like pudding that needs to be constantly stirred so it won't burn. I stirred a lot and didn't suffer in silence. The love and support we have for each other helped us work together on projects, ideas, and plans for our future.

Medicine has been the frame to the picture of our lives, but the words of our wedding song continue to inspire us in retirement:

*Moon River...we're off to see the world...we're after the same rainbow's end, waitin' round the bend, my huckleberry friend... and me.*

Be good to yourself and enjoy the stories that follow.

Kay Ashcraft

# Acknowledgements

For years, I promised patients, colleagues, family and friends that I would write a book about my experiences as a rural generalist family physician. Since I completed that book, *Reflections of a Country Doctor,* many encouraged me to write another book with more of my stories about my early life and my experiences as a doctor in the trenches of rural America. Since another single book could never tell a complete story, I have settled for *more* of the story that you will find in this book.

There are so many individuals who have made a difference in my life that I could not possibly list them all. I am forever grateful to all the teachers, coaches, professors, and friends I met along my life's journey who became, usually unknowingly, my surrogate mothers and fathers. All the people who allowed me to care for them gave me lasting memories. Just a few of the memories are relived in my books.

I owe a debt of gratitude to a special group of individuals, Richard and Mary Woods, Diane Cross, Bridget Ashcraft, Earl Neff, Doctor Curtis Holzgang, and Frank Newman, who read my text and offered editing suggestions along with constructive criticism.

Hugs and kisses are due to my children, Jennifer, Becky, and David, who encouraged me to write more of my stories.

My daughter Becky entered all my hospital patients into a computer database when she was a college student so I wouldn't forget my patients or their stories. That database, along with my charts and my memory, is the backbone for these stories. She not only edited my text and added constructive advice, but also worked on the jacket design.

There is one person who has been at my side through most of the parts in the book from high school through medical school

and from practicing medicine to writing in retirement: my wife
Kay. She knows many of my stories. She has read and edited the
entire manuscript multiple times. Her suggestions have
absolutely made my stories better.

# Author's Note

The stories in this book are true. I have done my best to portray the episodes as accurately as my memory and my records would allow. To protect people's confidentiality, I have changed the names of most of the individuals, my patients, their families, and my colleagues. In a few instances, I did change minor details that might identify certain people or places.

No pessimist ever discovered the secret of the stars,
or sailed to an uncharted land,
or opened a new doorway for the human spirit.

Benjamin Franklin

# Prologue

To say the least, my three brothers and I had difficult child-hoods. We became our own band of brothers just to survive. We had a mother and a father but not a real mom and dad. Our family moved often for reasons that, to this day, remain unclear to us. When I graduated from high school, I had lived in at least seventeen locations, and attended eight different schools. My father suffered from alcoholism, and our family members were forced to witness and endure the consequences of an alcoholic's behavior. My mother was mentally and physically slow, which doctors later determined to be related to a chronic thyroid condition. In modern terms, my family would be labeled, among other things, severely financially challenged with dysfunctional attributes (which means that we were really poor and really messed up).

During my youth, I sustained numerous, potentially fatal illnesses and injuries. These events provoked one physician to wonder if I really didn't have nine lives just like a cat. (This expression comes from a cat's excellent sense of balance and its ability to upright itself to land on its feet.)

In retrospect, it is truly amazing to me that my brothers and I survived to adulthood at all. We are living proof of the durability of the human body, mind, and spirit.

My parents obtained a set of the Collier's Encyclopedia when I was in the third grade. I loved it. I read the books for hours at a time. By my high school years, I had read most, if not all, of the entire set.

In the fifth grade, I saw and used a microscope for the first time. I learned about a Dutch shopkeeper named Antony van Leeuwenhoek (1632-1723) who invented the microscope in the 1600s. Soon afterward, I researched Leeuwenhoek in our encyclopedia. I wrote a report on the man, the microscope, which he had not invented but perfected, and the little animals he discovered that he called *beasties*. It still amazes me that Leeuwenhoek constructed a new microscope for each of his specimens, over five hundred in all.

Junior high school brought biology classes into my world. I learned about Louis Pasteur (1822-1895) and his work with germs. Interestingly, his discoveries occurred more than 100 years *after* van Leeuwenhoek, and I wondered why. Pasteur's discoveries saved the dairy and wine industries in France by introducing a germ-killing process now called pasteurization. Additionally, his work with germs helped to substantially decrease the number deaths after childbirth from infection. Pasteur also discovered ways to vaccinate against anthrax and tetanus, two common deadly diseases of man and animal at the time.

World history in junior high school introduced me to diseases and wars. In particular, I discovered Robert Koch (1843-1910), a Prussian genius who taught himself to read by the age of five. As a physician and microbiologist, he hunted for and uncovered the causes and treatments for some common diseases of his time including anthrax, tuberculosis, and cholera. I learned about Joseph Lister (1827-1912), an English surgeon who applied Pasteur's germ theories to surgery. He discovered that using carbolic acid to clean surgical tools and to wash hands and surgical wounds markedly reduced post-operative deaths from infections. Lister's work formed the foundation for modern surgical antiseptic procedures. Additionally, I was intrigued with yellow fever, a viral disease spread by mosquitoes. This disease severely hampered efforts to construct the Panama Canal until 1900 when an American soldier named Walter Reed discovered its cause and a treatment.

While completing a student athletic trainer's course at the age of twelve, I decided that I wanted to be a doctor. Except for my teacher at the time, most folks thought I was daydreaming. Not many kids from the south side of Billings, Montana, went off to become doctors. Heck, many of these kids never finished high school. My parents did not finish high school nor had any of their fifteen brothers and sisters. Many of my one hundred or more cousins did not graduate from high school.

The knowledge I acquired in my biology, chemistry, and physics classes in high school only amplified my excitement for the science of medicine. However, I believe my most motivating class was American history in my sophomore year of high school. My teacher described in detail how the implementation of sanitation systems, expanded vaccination programs, and improved personal hygiene in the early part of the 1900s dramatically reduced childhood mortality and almost doubled the average life expectancy in America by the middle of the twentieth century.

On a spring afternoon in April of my junior year in high school, I was asked to play in a softball game. At the game, I met a young lady named Kay who soon became my best girl and, after a few years, my wife. After more than forty-six years together, she remains my best friend and confidant.

Nearing graduation from Billings Senior High School in 1966, I did not have a dime to my name. However, a counselor at Senior High School believed in me and worked hard to get for me a small scholarship for which I had not applied. After some research, I determined that I could use the scholarship money to enroll at Eastern Montana College, a local liberal arts college. If I worked, I figured that I could make it through two years of school at Eastern before I would have to transfer to a larger school to improve my chances of getting accepted into a medical school. According to high school advisors at the time, that was how Montana kids got into medical school.

I was one of perhaps three hundred students in the premed curriculum when college started in the fall of 1966. After two quarters of calculus, physics, chemistry, and comparative anatomy, I was the last premed student standing.

During my college years, I usually worked two or three jobs at a time (one to pay for college, one to earn money for my family, and finally one to save money for medical school). Fortunately, I performed well enough in college to be accepted to the University of Oregon Medical School.

In medical school, I unearthed a boundless arena for learning outside of the classroom. During my free time, excursions to the emergency room, obstetrics, the cardiac intensive care unit, and the newborn intensive care unit provided me with marvelous hands-on experiences that I would use in later years. In the medical school library I renewed my interest with some old friends including Lister, Pasteur, van Leeuwenhoek, and Koch. I found other medical greats that enthralled me including Crawford Long, M.D., the first to use general anesthesia for surgery in 1842, William Worral Mayo and his sons, William and Charles, who expanded the work of Lister and Long to perpetuate the specialty of surgery, Sir William Osler, the master of observation and diagnosis, and Jonas Salk, the founder of the polio vaccine.

I was in the group of medical school graduates who experienced the last of the Ironman internships. After my class graduated, the permitted number of training hours for new doctors-in-training was reduced substantially. Many in medicine think the politicians and the educators made a mistake with these changes.

After my medical training, my family and I moved to Lusk, Wyoming, a small town in the southeastern part of the state, where I served in the National Health Service Corps with Doctor William Berryman, a medical school classmate.

Afterward, we moved north to northeastern Montana and a town named Sidney. I started practicing medicine there on my birthday in the spring of 1976. Even though my wife Kay and I planned to stay in Sidney only one year, I closed my office on my birthday exactly twenty-five years later.

Thereafter, Kay and I moved to Billings, Montana, where I was a member of the faculty of the Montana Family Medicine Residency Program for five years. I helped to develop this training program some years before.

While appreciating the worldwide information explosion, one of my medical school professors cautioned our class with, "Remember that half of what you learn today in medical school will be wrong in five years." In retrospect, I think his timeline was too long. I've witnessed the development of diagnostic tools like CAT scans, MRIs, PET scans, ultrasounds, mammography, micro-technique blood testing for newborns, and more. All of these technologies were made possible by advances in computer technology. Mega-computers have enabled researchers to delineate the human genetic codes in a matter of months instead of a few generations.

Inserting stents (small tubes) into heart arteries to keep them open now replaces many heart bypass surgeries which were "the thing" when I trained. Organ transplantation has become commonplace. Many surgical procedures are now done through hollow instruments such as laparoscopes, arthroscopes, and gastroscopes.

When I started medical school, the <u>Physician's Desk Reference</u> (PDR), a commonly used medication reference book, was about one inch thick with large print. The book has expanded in size to almost three inches thick with small print. Most of the medications that are commonplace today for anesthesia, hypertension, heart failure, fluid control, diabetes, cancer, mental illness, and many other ailments did not exist when I was in medical school.

I have witnessed the practice of medicine evolve from a predominately private practice-based system to an employer-based system. The calling of medicine I knew and cherished has evolved into the business of medicine. The government, through programs like Medicare, Medicaid, Workers' Compensation, and others, has replaced the individual as the primary payer source for most hospital and physician services. In the view of many, the development of third-party payers and the escalation of liability insurance costs have placed a wedge between the physician and his patient. Sadly, I have witnessed the philanthropy of physicians decline dramatically too.

In 1994, a retiring surgeon told me that, in his forty years in medicine, he had seen a change in the patient's expectations toward major surgery from "Will I survive?" to "How long will I be laid up?" to "I have to be back to work on Monday, or else!"

Indeed, many things changed during my career in medicine, some for the better and some not. Despite these changes, however, one constant remains: people continue to need medical assistance with their illnesses and their injuries.

This book spans my experiences from my early childhood through my clinical years. Like my previous book, *Reflections of a Country Doctor*, this book is about reality; it is about events in our collective lives that happen to our friends and our neighbors daily.

I hope you enjoy the journey.

The practice of medicine will be very much as you make it -
to one a worry, a care, a perpetual annoyance;
to another, a daily job and a life of as much happiness and usefulness
as can well fall to the lot of man, because it is a life of self-sacrifice
and of countless opportunities to comfort and help the weak-hearted,
and to raise up those that fall.

Sir William Osler, M.D.

# Premed

"Do what you can, with what you have, where you are."

Theodore Roosevelt

# Tommy

My family moved to Albuquerque, New Mexico, from
Arkansas in the summer of 1952 after the birth of my youngest
brother. (I would learn later that this was already my seventh
home.) When I was five years old, I befriended a neighbor named
Tommy Rodriguez. When I started school at Lavaland Elementary the next year, Tommy was going to be in my classroom.

Mrs. Rowell was our first grade teacher. From my perspective
as a six-year-old boy, she was scary. She seemed tall and slim to
me, but I noticed that the male teachers were much bigger than
she. Mrs. Rowell appeared old with her wrinkled facial skin and
her gray hair pulled into a bun on the back of her head. She
always wore a long dress down to her ankles and black shoes that
looked like boots with hooks for leather laces. Finally, she always
carried a pointer stick with a metal point.

Every morning our class lined up on the playground and
marched into our room while the song "Soldier Boy" played on
her record player. Once inside, and after attendance had been
taken, our class recited the Pledge of Allegiance. This was always
followed by one of three songs: "The Star-spangled Banner,"
"America," or "America the Beautiful."

Most days I walked to school with my older brother Jay.
Tommy and I would meet on the playground and have some fun
in the mornings before school started and during recesses. We
were best buddies.

One fall morning Tommy did not come to school. When he was
absent a second day, I went to his home after school to see him.
His mother told me that Tommy was sick and that I could see
him when he got better. Tommy missed school the rest of the
week.

One day the following week, Mrs. Rowell told our class that
Tommy was very sick and that we should all pray for him to get
better. She may have told us what was wrong with my friend, but
I do not recall. I do remember that Mrs. Rowell brought to school
a flower in a pot that she wanted the class to care for until
Tommy was well enough to take it home. Our collective job was
to water the flower every day. She placed the pot on Tommy's
desk where it would stay until he could take it home.

Sometime later Mrs. Rowell told our class that Tommy had polio and was going to be sick a long time. She asked us to help his family pay their medical bills by collecting money for the March of Dimes.

I remember going home and getting a tin can from the garbage. My mother caught me in the act of rummaging through the garbage and asked me what I was doing. I told my mom about Tommy and the March of Dimes. She then found me a metal cup with a handle, cleaned it, and threw my dirty tin can away. I went out many times collecting dimes for Tommy.

In 1954, a vaccine for polio was undergoing trials. In April 1955, the success of the vaccine was reported nationally, and a nationwide polio immunization campaign started.

In the spring of 1955, there was a big immunization event for polio in Albuquerque. The fire engines went through the neighborhoods with loud speakers announcing the event. Police cars did the same. On a Saturday morning my parents packed their four kids into the car and took us down to the city events center to get immunized against polio. There were hundreds, perhaps thousands, of kids in various states of terror as they anticipated the injection for polio, a disease they, and their parents, knew little to nothing about.

Just before school let out for the year, my classmates and I lined up on the playground in the morning as usual. However, on this day, Mrs. Rowell was not present to greet us. In her place was another female teacher. Otherwise, our routine this morning was the same.

When Mrs. Rowell came into our classroom a short time later, someone asked why she was crying.

She just pointed to Tommy's desk. Our potted flower was gone. A single yellow flower had replaced it. Mrs. Rowell then told us that Tommy had died from his polio.

I do not remember what, if anything, Mrs. Rowell said afterward because I started to cry. I think I cried the rest of that day. After school, I told my mom about Tommy; she cried too. (My mom lost a baby girl during childbirth earlier that year.)

My family moved from the neighborhood soon after the school year ended. I missed Tommy all summer and into the second grade. My father showed little sympathy and told me to, "Quit blubbering and act like a man." I was only seven years old.

Fortunately for me, my second grade teacher, Mrs. Benton, understood and gave me hugs everyday for a long time.

# A Hard Head

I got my first bicycle when I was about five years old. I was always a curious sort and enjoyed tinkering with just about anything mechanical. Before I was in the first grade, I was able to dismantle my bicycle and then put it back together, usually without having any leftover pieces or losing any of my dad's tools. I particularly liked to lower the handlebars so I could get more power when pedaling. Also, I attached playing cards to the rear fender crossbar with clothespins so that the cards would strike the wheel spokes and make noise like a motorcycle when I rode. I thought I was really cool! My friend Tommy and I would ride our bikes as much as we could.

The street by our home had a small incline, but for a small kid like me it was a hill! I had come down this hill many times without concerns. The traffic on our street always seemed nonexistent during the day. I would ride my way to the top of the hill only to turn around and speed back down. Usually, I could play like this for hours and still be within range to hear my mom when she called me.

One day when I was about six years old, I fixed up my bike with lowered handlebars and noisemaking cards on the wheels so I was really *neat*. I rode my bike to the top of the hill and headed downward. When I was about halfway down the hill, a car backed out of a driveway in front of me. Almost immediately I hit the back of the car and became airborne. I struck the back window with my head and fell to the ground when the car drove away.

I do not know how long I lay on the ground. Nobody came by to help me. When I finally became oriented, I had a really sore head. I was crying, and blood was streaming down my face. Worse yet, the front wheel of my bike was twisted, and the wheel fork was bent. I dragged my bike several blocks to my home.

My mom wanted to know what happened. However, when I told her, she thought I was telling a story because I guess she assumed I was doing something I wasn't supposed to be doing. My mom placed something on my head to stop the bleeding. She then called the doctor.

Doctor P.E. Wally (I remember his name because it was printed on the side of his doctor's bag) came to our house later that day. I remember that he put some stitches in my head. I was told not to go out to play for a few days. I probably was diagnosed with a concussion.

When my dad came home from work, I had to tell him my trauma story. I took him to the accident scene, and he saw my blood on the ground. He told me that nobody lived in the house where the car came out.

My dad made fun of me afterward because I had a scab on my forehead and a black eye. He said I looked like a palooka.

Before long I got a new bicycle. I tuned it up so that I could look neat again when I rode down the hill.

A similar event occurred when I was about nine years old when we lived in the northeastern part of Albuquerque. My friend Paul Kessler told me that his church was having a "bring a friend" day and asked me to go to Sunday school with him. I rode my bike to meet him at his church, which was not far from our homes. After the church gathering, I started to ride home. I was a few blocks from my home riding on the left side of the street so I faced traffic. This was a trick I learned after my first crash. A car came around a corner from behind me, crossed onto my side of the street, and hit me! My bike and I flew into the curb, and I catapulted onto the sidewalk. The car did not stop. Again, I made a one-point landing on my head.

I do not know how long it was before a passing car stopped and the driver got out to help me. The man noticed that I had hit my head and had blood streaming down my face. Somehow, the fellow got my bike and me home.

I don't remember much more of that day except Doctor Wally came to see me at my home. He didn't put any stitches into my head this time. However, I had to stay inside for a day or so. This time my bike fared better; it just had a few scratches and a flat tire.

Doctor Wally told me that it was good that I had a hard head!

# Dimples and Stripes

Sometime during the fourth grade I noticed that the girl who sat across from me had facial dimples when she smiled. After that day, I became intrigued with dimples. I noticed that a good number of my other schoolmates had dimples when they smiled. My teacher, Mrs. Cloud, also had dimples. In addition, they all had dimples on *both* sides of their faces.

When I looked into the mirror, I saw a dimple only on the right side of my face. Try as I might, I could not smile big enough to produce a second dimple on the left side of my face. This was just a curiosity to me until I asked my mom and dad one day about my dimple.

My mom told me, "You don't have dimples. You fell on your head when you were a baby and damaged your face."

My dad said, "You fell off the second story porch at your grandma's house and landed on a pile of bricks. One of the bricks broke your cheek. That dimple is a scar from the bricks."

My mother added, "You were knocked out, and you slept for three days. I was worried sick, but Grandma Ashcraft said you would wake up when it was time. And you did."

I didn't appreciate the significance of this explanation at the time. I just accepted the fact that I had only one dimple. (Now I know that I was in a coma for three days!)

During my first year at Eastern Montana College, I took classes in water safety and became certified to teach swimming and to be a lifeguard. The summer after my freshman year I worked as a lifeguard and a swimming instructor at the Rose Park pool in Billings, Montana. Like all lifeguards of my era, I did not use sunscreens for skin protection. The idea of commercial sunscreens wasn't around. We had tanning lotions. I spent twelve hours a day in the sun wearing nothing more than a swimming suit, and I developed an incredibly dark suntan.

Sometime in July one of the other lifeguards noticed that I seemed to have darker colored stripes like a zebra on my legs. When I got home and looked at myself in a mirror, I could see the lines on my chest, abdomen, thighs, and feet. I thought I just tanned unevenly. My skin appeared as if I had been barbecued.

I displayed my interesting tan to my mom. She told me that I had fallen on a space heater just after I had learned to walk. We lived in Shelby, Montana, at the time. She explained that it was a cold winter and several small space heaters were all they had to heat the apartment where we lived. After my accident, my parents had a doctor come to the apartment to examine me; he wanted to put me in the hospital. However, my parents had no money to pay hospital bills. My mom told me that the doctor gave her some "black stuff" to put on the burns. He gave her instructions for changing bandages and suggested that she pray for me. Apparently, the burns were extensive enough for the doctor to be concerned for my survival.

My mother continued to tell me that she changed bandages on my burns for almost four months. In the beginning she threw up each time she changed the bandages. (She was also pregnant at the time.) My mom demonstrated for me how the burned skin peeled off and how she had to clean the burns before the "black stuff" could be reapplied. She explained how she cried with each bandage change because I screamed with pain. Then, without any emotion, my mom said, "You didn't die. You got better."

Near the end of the hot summer of 1967, I joined the rest of my family in Hensley, Arkansas, for my grandparents' fiftieth wedding anniversary. My relatives were unsure if I was part of the same family. I was so dark and the rest of my family was so white, like them! I met my grandparents in the kitchen one morning while they made breakfast. I asked the pair about what they knew about my dimple and my stripes.

My grandpa said, "Boy, you darn near kilt yursef. You tumbled off that high porch yonder (pointing toward another nearby building) onto a pile of rocks and landed on yur haid. You hurt yursef real bad. You slep for days before you come to. Yur gramma prayed fur ya day and night."

My grandmother chimed in with, "I tolt your mom that you would be all right, and you would wake up when the good Lord said so. She was young. I din't want to let her know how worried we all was. You finally woke up after three days."

Grandpa finished with, "You've had that dent in your cheek ever since."

I asked them what they knew, if anything, about my burns since it happened when we lived in Montana.

Grandma said all she knew was from the letters written by Rachelle (my mom). "Rachelle said the doctor tolt her that you might die 'cause you was burnt so bad." Grandma told me she asked all the relatives to pray for me. Then she said, "And just look at ya now, all growed up and all."

I displayed my scars. Grandpa, who could not see well, stated, "Boy, looks like you went and got yursef barbecued!" He then chuckled out loud.

# A Hero

All children need good role models. For most kids, the job of being a role model usually belongs to their parents. Usually, the girls have their mother, and the boys have their father. In the case of my brothers and me, our alcoholic father proved to be a negative role model. That is, I wanted *not* to be like my father. My feelings only intensified as I grew older. My parents seemed to have little interest in us boys or what we did. In response to their apparent indifference toward us, we fended for ourselves to a large extent. We four boys became our own band of brothers to survive.

The summer before I was to enter the fifth grade, our family moved to Billings, Montana, with stays in Denver, Colorado, the home of my dad's sister, and Havre, Montana, the home of my mom's siblings.

In the sixth grade, our physical education teacher introduced our class to John, a teacher at the high school who was interested in coaching wrestling. John was a large man with monstrous muscles. I wanted to be just like John. Of course, I was smaller than my classmates. I was a seventy-pound weakling.

Our class could not be a real team yet, but John offered to teach us to wrestle during off-school hours. The only time we could use the gym was at 7 a.m. before school started. I did not miss a session. Each day after we showered, I would talk with John about anything. He always made time for me, was always courteous, and told me where to seek answers to my queries that he could not answer. John never spoke of himself or his family. His time at the school was for us.

During the eighth grade, John arranged for our school to send a wrestling team to the city junior high school wrestling championships. All the wrestlers had to be weighed to determine their weight class. My weight was less than the lowest class, so I wrestled with heavier kids. John always told us, "It's not the size of the dog in the fight. It's the size of the fight in the dog."

I won the city wrestling championship in the lowest weight class that year. Neither of my parents came to watch me compete or to share in my excitement about winning. However, John was there. He drove me home after the tournament; we celebrated with an ice cream cone at a local drive-in.

My family moved often afterward for reasons that still remain unknown to me. We lived in six homes in four cities over the next five years. We ended up in Billings where we started, just in a different house. I was now a junior at the Billings Senior High School, and John was the boys' counselor and assistant dean of boys. John noticed that I had grown some since he had seen me last. (I grew twelve inches in height over the previous summer!)

I met with John formally every few months to talk about my plans for the future. I told him that I wanted to be a doctor, but I was as poor as a church mouse. I had the brains but not the cash. John remained supportive and encouraged me to do my best. We never talked about my home life, but somehow, I think he knew without asking. John and I met and exchanged greetings often in the hallways during class changes.

During the fall quarter, I met John at the concession stand during a football game. I asked him why he wasn't watching the game. He said simply, "They need me more here." I learned later that John had been the school's head football coach, and one of his players died from head injuries sustained during a game.

I asked him about the player's death during one of my counseling meetings. He became tearful and replied, "I just couldn't coach after he died."

John remained my role model and my hero.

As a senior, I decided to try out for the cross-country team now that I had grown and was stronger. I did okay and made the varsity squad. Our team won the state title that year. Neither of my parents ever saw me run. John, on the other hand, called me into his office after the state meet to offer his congratulations.

During my senior year, the local Rotary Club selected me as a student of the month. Parents were encouraged to accompany their children; my parents did not come. I informed John I could not go to the luncheon because I had no escort. He changed his schedule and went with me.

In the spring, I joined the track team. At one relay race in Wyoming, a teammate and I ran the fastest half-mile races yet for that season, 2:00 and 1:59. Our distance relay teams established five meet records that day; I came home with five gold medals. My parents paid no attention. On Monday, John gave me a pat on the back.

The morning of the awards assembly before graduation, I received separate awards for science and physics. Near the end of the program I was awarded a scholarship for which I had not applied. This scholarship would allow me to begin college. Afterward, John came up to me and said, "I worked hard to get that scholarship. Now, make us proud." He put his hand on my shoulder and shook my hand. John was the dad I never had.

Many years later, I learned that John had been elected to the Wyoming Athletic Hall of Fame. In the newspaper article I learned that he had been the first Wyoming football player ever to be named an all-American. In addition, he had received all-conference awards four consecutive years in baseball and football. There was a listing of the state, regional, and national awards he had received over the years. Yet, John never mentioned them to me.

After reading the article, I wrote John a letter to tell him about my life's journey since high school. In finishing, I told John that over the years my wife and I had converted the $500 scholarship he obtained for me into scholarships for five hundred kids. I wrote, "I hope I made you proud."

I received a call from John about a week later. He told me he gave the letter to his wife and they cried together.

John died on New Year's Day 2008 at the age of eighty-five.

He was my hero.

# Spring Quarter

My second year in premed was going well. Academically, I was near the top of my class. I had two part-time jobs to pay the bills. That fall, our cross-country team won its second consecutive conference title. I finished in fourth place at the conference meet.

All was going well until mid-March of 1968. I had just finished running my personal best times at three miles and six miles on a Wednesday. The following Friday morning I could barely walk because of leg pain. A physician who thought I had a pulled muscle from overuse examined me and gave me instructions not to run for a couple of weeks. On Saturday, however, I had a fever of 104 degrees, and I could not walk. I was carried from my home by an ambulance crew and transported to a local hospital. The same physician admitted me to the hospital from the emergency room. He now diagnosed bacterial septicemia and shock.[1] I spent the next three weeks in a Billings hospital with a strange blood infection that almost killed me. Neither the doctors nor I had any idea how I could have contracted the disease. Fortunately the doctors had a new penicillin product that killed the bug. It just took 100 injections in my butt, one shot every four hours for seventeen days! I also received an injection of morphine for pain, four times a day for fifteen days. When I left the hospital, I could walk, but barely. I had shrunk down to 120 pounds.

To compound my concerns, I was three weeks behind in my college studies for the spring quarter, and I was behind in my work obligations. My college advisor suggested that I stay out of school a year and start my second year over.

I declined.

I was on a mission to be a doctor. Besides, I still had to take the medical college admission test (MCAT) in a few months to see if I could even qualify for medical school.

I talked with my science professors and my employers about a schedule for making up my delayed work and studies. They were more than accommodating.

---

[1] Septicemia is a generic term for a blood infection. Shock is a physiologic state in which the blood pressure drops and the circulatory system fails to maintain adequate perfusion of the vital organs. Septic shock is often fatal.

About a week after being back at school, I was in the chemistry lab making up a required experiment for organic chemistry. It was a time of day when no labs were scheduled. After mixing the first two chemicals, smoke started to arise from the mixing flask. Within moments, the entire project exploded. The next thing I recall is that someone was yelling for tourniquets. Soon thereafter, I was carried down the stairs to an awaiting car that transported me to the hospital emergency room. After an evaluation, I was back in a hospital. This time I was being surgically repaired, a process that I was told took about three hours.

My surgeon told me the next morning that he repaired my right axillary artery and vein,[2] reattached my right ring finger, removed twenty-three pieces of glass from various body areas, and sutured a lot of holes. In addition, he told me that he had a former classmate who had attempted the same experiment in a college back east a few months before and was killed in the explosion.

A short time after my accident, the chemistry professors repeated the experiment outdoors with similar results. My presumed safe experiment was removed from the required list of experiments. (My damaged safety goggles and my bloody clothes remained on display outside the chemistry labs for about twenty-five years as a reminder to students to use proper safety equipment.) After I returned to school, I was told that I was the only student to ever really blow up the chemistry lab at Eastern Montana College. As far as I know, I may still hold that dubious honor.

Worse yet, another week in class and work were wasted while I was hospitalized. I was now four weeks behind in a ten-week quarter. Again, I met with the faculty. Each faculty member and lab assistant wanted to help me succeed. However, the odds were definitely against me. I came to school early, I left late, and I came in on weekends. I rested between classes and between lab sessions. A faculty member or a lab assistant was always available to help me when I needed them. By the end of the quarter I had made up all the missed class work. The chemistry department gave me credit for performing additional lab experiments. I was just a bit gun shy when I walked into the chemistry labs.

Just before finals week, I decided to try jogging again. I was running slowly without much pain until I made the turn at the

---

[2] The axillary artery and vein are the primary vascular tributaries in the axilla that provide blood to and from the arm and hand.

corner of Poly Drive and Virginia Lane next to the college. A hit-and-run yellow Volkswagen bug hit me from behind. I made my third trip to the emergency room in eight weeks! This time, however, I was just bruised and scraped. The emergency room physician wanted to know how many lives I had left.

To say the least, I had had a bad spring quarter.

At the time, the first two years of premedical studies at a smaller college, in my case Eastern Montana College (EMC), were meant to be used merely as a stepping stone to another larger college to earn an undergraduate degree before going to medical school. My situation had changed. Faculty from the chemistry and physics departments suggested that I earn a degree from EMC and then go straight to medical school. Also, the professors were curious about how well they were preparing their students for the basic sciences part of medical school. *Besides, as far as they knew, no one had ever done it.*

I took my Medical College Admission Test (MCAT) that summer and scored well.

Two years later I graduated from Eastern Montana College with high honors.

I would be amiss not to mention that I graduated at the peak of the Vietnam War. Fortunately for me, my draft lottery number was not picked in 1968, 1969, or 1970, and I was allowed the privilege to finish college. Unfortunately, at least ten of my high school and college classmates had already been killed in the war. On that day in May 1970, a somber graduation ceremony was held outside on the lawn by the gymnasium. Many of my classmates walked up the steps on the south side of the stage to receive their diplomas and then walked over to the north side where they received their draft notices at the base of the steps. I knew they would be in Viet Nam by the end of the summer.

Charles Dickens described the situation well in 1859 when he wrote in <u>A Tale of Two Cities</u>:

> *"It was the best of times, it was the worst of times;*
> *it was the age of wisdom, it was the age of foolishness;*
> *it was the epoch of belief, it was the epoch of incredulity;*
> *it was the season of Light, it was the season of Darkness;*
> *it was the spring of hope, it was the winter of despair;*

*we had everything before us, we had nothing before us;
we were all going directly to Heaven, we were all going
the other way."*

I was the first graduate of Eastern Montana College to attend
and graduate from a medical school.

I graduated from the University of Oregon Medical School.

# Medical School

You *may* cure a patient rarely.
You *may* improve a patient occasionally.
But, you *will* aid and comfort a patient always.

Howard P. Lewis, M.D.
Professor of Medicine,
University of Oregon Medical School

# Say What?

Research scientists who spend their lives in laboratories evaluating information and developing experiments also give many lectures in medical schools. These professionals are quite good in their respective areas of expertise. However, many of them are most uncomfortable speaking before groups, especially groups of intelligent people like medical students. The research scientists who were extracted from the friendly confines of their laboratories in my medical school to present lectures to my medical school class about their narrow areas of expertise were no different.

My second-year medical school class had endured lectures for six to eight hours a day, five days a week for several months without a significant break. One Friday morning my class sat through a series of incredibly dull physiology lectures. That afternoon our second lecturer was a gastrointestinal physiologist[3] from somewhere in Britain. He spoke with a heavy accent that made his speech difficult for many of us to understand. A few minutes into the presentation, the lecturer said something caused "inna stynal hooey" in the human bowel.

A few hands rose, but the lecturer paid little attention and continued with his slide show and his prepared remarks. After another few minutes, the instructor repeated the term "inna stynal hooey." This time, more hands raised as the students tried to find some clarification of the lecturer's comments. Again, the lecturer continued with his comments.

By now, the students were whispering among themselves asking, "What is 'inna stynal hooey'?"

Not only was this instructor's accent difficult to understand, but also he used colloquial terms that made little sense to us. Soon, many of the students were no longer paying attention to the presentation.

When the lecturer said "inna stynal hooey" again, a bewildered medical student in the lower rows of the auditorium stood up in front of the lecturer and asked, "Sir, what the heck is 'inna stynal hooey'?"

---

[3] A gastrointestinal physiologist studies the biologic functioning of the human intestinal tract and its associated organs including the liver, pancreas, stomach, and gallbladder.

The lecturer was taken aback and appeared somewhat shaken after his rhetorical rhythm was disrupted. With his strong British accent, he asked, "Young man, would you please repeat your question?"

The medical student stated loudly, "Sir, I am confused. What is 'inna stynal hooey'?"

Before the presenter could respond, a voice from the back of the auditorium yelled, "He's saying *intestinal hurry*. He's talking about diarrhea." The medical student then yelled, "He's saying somebody has the shits – just like this lecture is!"

At this point the entire class started to laugh. Professional decorum was thrown out the window. After weeks of constant concentration, the members of my medical school class needed a mental break. This was that moment.

Our class became unruly, but the physiologist acted as if nothing was happening in the audience. He finished his presentation on time and then strutted off the stage.

Two more lectures followed that afternoon, but most of us heard little. We took a mental recess!

# A Secret

Agnes was my very first patient when I started my outpatient clinic rotation in internal medicine. She was a petite woman in her late seventies who came to the general medicine clinic complaining of severe back and leg pain. The pains had been present for months. Because of the discomfort, Agnes could no longer function well at home. This elderly woman told me that she had been healthy her entire life. She took no medicines. She went to doctors only in desperation. She denied having any major illnesses, injuries, or operations. Agnes became a widow soon after World War I ended.

After I interviewed Agnes, I performed a complete physical examination (which was required of all visits to allow medical students the opportunity to develop their examination skills). Agnes thought that my examining her eyes and throat was a curious way to evaluate back pain, but she was patient and endured my efforts. After the examination, I left the room to consult with my preceptor for the morning.

Doctor Karl Burger was our volunteer preceptor for the day. He was an internist with over thirty years experience in private practice. After I presented Agnes' history and my physical examination findings to Doctor Burger, we decided that Agnes most likely had degenerative arthritis of her back and hips as the cause of her pain. However, to determine the severity of her disease, Doctor Burger and I elected to obtain X-rays of her back and hips. Additionally, since she had not seen a physician in more than forty years, we decided to obtain some blood for a few screening lab tests.

When Agnes returned from the radiology department with her x-rays, I left her in the examination room while Doctor Burger and I reviewed her films in the consultation area. When I put the first film onto the viewing screen, Doctor Burger asked me excitedly, "Do you see that?"

I was just a medical student on my first day in real clinical medicine. I knew basic science, but I knew little of clinical medicine. In addition, I had never seriously looked at an x-ray. I just said, "No."

Doctor Burger asked me to put up more of the x-rays. He just looked at the black-and-white pictures and became increasingly giddy with excitement. Finally, he prodded me into action with, "Young Doctor Ashcraft, tell me what you see."

I started by describing the anatomy of the spine and the abnormalities that I thought I saw on the x-rays.

Doctor Burger allowed me to continue for a short time before he said, "She has degenerative arthritis in her back and hips. What else do you see?"

I always disliked the, "What am I thinking?" game that was played so often in medical school. I just responded with, "I don't know."

Doctor Burger then took my hand, grabbed my index finger, and placed it on the film that showed a side view of the woman's spine. There was a spot that appeared white and was located in the soft tissue in the area of the buttock. On the frontal view films of the pelvis, there were spots in the soft tissues of both buttocks. Doctor Burger now asked me, "What is that?"

I told him I had no idea.

He exclaimed, "This woman has syphilis!"

Now I was really confused. My patient came in because of back and leg pain, and now my preceptor tells me she has syphilis in her butt! Things were not adding up. I asked Doctor Burger how he knew this woman had syphilis.

He replied, "I will bet you that those are bismuth deposits in her backside. Bismuth was a common treatment for syphilis before antibiotics were discovered." Then he said, "By God, a diagnosis of syphilis because of metal in the ass! Doctor Ashcraft, you've made my day!" Doctor Burger asked me to return to my patient and expand my history to include venereal diseases.

I returned to the examination room and told Agnes about the spots on her x-rays. She started to whimper. While holding back tears, she told me her story of a young girl who married her prince charming soon before he went off to Europe to fight in World War I. She remained faithful while her husband was gone. Soon after his return home, Agnes said she noticed a painless sore on her genitalia. She was diagnosed with syphilis, which she got from her husband. (He apparently had had affairs with infected French women.) She received a series of bismuth injections for the infection.

Agnes told me that her husband died several years after the war in an accident. She never remarried. Being terribly embarrassed and humiliated, Agnes told nobody about her disease. Only she and her doctor knew the real story. Being infected with syphilis became her lifelong secret.

I returned to the consultation room to find Doctor Burger sharing the x-rays with more medical students, medical residents, and other preceptors. When I entered the room, he asked with excitement, "What did she say?"

I said, "She was treated for syphilis in 1919."

Doctor Burger exclaimed, "By God, I knew it!" He then directed me to obtain an infectious disease consultation for Agnes ASAP (as soon as possible).

I called the infectious disease resident on duty. Within minutes a team of physicians from the infectious disease department, including the department chief, arrived. After I introduced the other doctors to Agnes, they escorted her away to be further scrutinized and treated for her syphilis.

I asked Doctor Burger about my patient's back and leg pains.

He assured me that her pain was related to the degenerative arthritis in her back and hips and not the syphilis. The only treatment at the time was heat, exercise, and pain medication.

When I arrived at the outpatient medicine clinic several weeks later, the nurse gave me a small package with a note attached. The nurse told me that an elderly woman had brought it to the clinic the day before.

The package contained a single piece of candy. The note said, "For one sweet boy who freed me from my secret. Thank you. Agnes."

# Surprise!

I had enjoyed visiting the emergency room at the Multnomah County Hospital in my free time since my earliest days of medical school. One of the in-house staff physicians always needed assistance from a willing medical student. Being available to help, I had the opportunity to insert intravenous catheters, apply casts, suture wounds, and observe major trauma care.

One weekend night in 1972, I was hanging out in the emergency room with the surgery resident when the ER intern came into the conference area to discuss a case. Just as he started to give the patient's history and complaints, we heard a shrieking scream coming from a room in the emergency room. The intern said, "That's my patient. She'll be okay for now."

He continued with his presentation for Martha Anderson, an obese fifty-three-year-old woman who had been having intermittent abdominal pain for over the previous two weeks. The pain was associated with nausea, poor appetite, and an upset stomach. The pain radiated from her back into her groin at different times. The woman denied any fever or chills. The woman's husband brought her to the emergency room because he was "tired of her whining." The intern noted that, "She is so fat I could not tell a thing from her abdominal exam." The intern's final assessment was that the woman was either passing a kidney stone or having a bad gallbladder attack. He thought the patient should be sent up to surgery on the third floor of the hospital for further evaluation and possibly surgery.

Hearing that he may get to do surgery, the surgical resident told the intern that he would meet him and the patient in the elevator after completing an errand. The intern asked me to accompany them to the surgery floor. He said, "Who knows, you might see some action tonight."

The intern advised the husband of his assessments and that his wife was being transferred to surgery on the third floor. The husband told us that his car was double-parked outside the emergency room door. He would go to the third floor after he found another parking location.

The intern and I loaded Martha onto a gurney and headed toward the elevator.

The surgical resident jumped into the elevator just as the door was closing, and the door caught his leg. The intern and I had to pry the doors open to release him. The woman let out another blood curdling scream. The surgical resident was surprised by the woman's agitation. He asked the woman, "How often do you have these pains?"

The woman responded, "Every few minutes! What's wrong with me Doctor?"

The resident surgeon sneered at the intern physician and said, "*That* was an important piece of history!"

The resident surgeon placed his hand on the woman's obese abdomen and said, "That's no gallbladder. This woman's pregnant. She's in labor. Let's get her to OB."

Hearing this conversation, the woman shouted, "That's impossible. I haven't had my monthly for over a year."

The resident said, "Mrs. Anderson, at your age, that may have been your last monthly. Right now, I think you're going to have a baby."

Outside the elevator on the third floor of the hospital, the surgical departments separated. To the left was general surgery; to the right was Ob/Gyn surgery.[4] We took our patient to the right. After the surgical resident spoke with the OB resident about our patient, the two ER physicians headed back to work. The OB resident asked me to hang around OB for a while. He said, "Who knows, maybe you'll learn something."

When I said I would stay, the OB resident directed me to the locker room to change into surgical attire. He encouraged me to hurry because he didn't think the patient was going to allow us much time. When I emerged from the locker room, a nurse escorted me promptly to a surgical suite where the OB resident had prepared our patient for a delivery. He asked me, "Have you ever delivered a baby?"

I replied, "Yes, sir." I continued by telling him the story of my first OB experience the previous summer when I helped a migrant woman deliver a breech nine-pound baby in a tent.

The OB resident said, "I'm impressed. I guess it's time for number two." He pulled my stool toward the mother's bottom as

---

[4] Ob/Gyn stands for a medical and surgical subspecialty of medicine that treats disorders of women including obstetrics, gynecology, and fertility.

he pushed himself aside. He then explained what and how I was going to do to deliver this baby. He showed me the instruments I would need, the way to apply sterile drapes, and how to evaluate the baby's head position by feeling the boney sutures of the skull.

The mother's contractions intensified, and after some encouragement from the OB resident, her screeching turned into purposeful grunting. As the baby's head emerged, the resident showed me how to suction the baby's mouth and nose *before* the infant took its first breath.[5] He explained why the baby had to be cleaned and dried promptly to prevent hypothermia and reduce stress.[6]

A large baby boy came out hollering. After I cleaned him off, the nurse took him to the infant warmer.

The resident discussed the delivery of the afterbirth and how to remove the placenta manually if the circumstances required it. This day, he had me remove the placenta manually just for the experience.

Amazingly, the instant her baby was born, the mom's pains and screaming stopped. A miracle!

Earlier, I thought that I might be deaf before the end of the day.

The OB resident showed me a technique to repair the lacerations the mother had incurred. He then moved aside and said, "You're on." I then repaired my first perineal laceration.[7]

The nurse called out, "The baby weighs ten pounds and four ounces! He's a whopper!"

I remember looking up at the woman's abdomen and thinking, "She looks a lot thinner now."

When all my work was completed, the new mom was transferred to a cart before going to a postpartum room. Our nurse showed the newborn boy to Martha and handed the child to a nursery attendant. The OB resident said, "I guess we had better find the dad."

---

[5] Suction of the newborn's nose and throat before the first breath helps to prevent the aspiration of any material that may be in the upper airway into the lungs. This maneuver should reduce lung infections in the newborn.

[6] Newborns can easily become hypothermic, a condition of a low body temperature, which increases the bodily stresses caused by the birth. Rapid drying and wrapping a newborn in a blanket are essential maneuvers to prevent hypothermia.

[7] The perineum is the tissue between the anus and the vaginal opening. This area is often injured during childbirth.

We found the husband down the hall in the surgery waiting area. The OB resident explained to him that his wife did not have a bad gallbladder; she had a baby. He was now the proud poppa of a ten-pound four-ounce baby boy.

The man's jaw dropped in disbelief. He exclaimed, "My God, we thought she was just going through the change. Hey, I'm fifty-eight years old. Our youngest grandchild is three. Oh my!"

We walked him down the hallway to the obstetrics wing to see his wife who was no longer in pain.

They just stared at one another for a few moments. Then she smiled and quipped, "Hey, Daddy. SURPRISE!"

# Oscar

As a third year medical student, my first clinical rotation was on the general medicine wing at the Multnomah County Hospital in Portland, Oregon. I chose this hospital for as many clinical rotations as possible because multiple outgoing students had told me the best experiences were to be found here.

The Multnomah County Hospital and its clinics provided the last place for the indigent population in Portland, Oregon, and the surrounding area to receive intensive medical care. Many of the patients suffered with the severe problems related to long-term alcohol and/or drug use. Many of the patients lived around and underneath the Burnside Bridge in the middle of downtown Portland. Many of our patients on the medical ward qualified for care in our medical intensive care unit (ICU). Unfortunately, the ICUs were usually filled to overflowing with patients who were even sicker. Political buzzwords today include rationing of care. The reality is that county medical facilities have rationed care for as long as they have had budgets. That is, forever.

Each medical team at the Multnomah County Hospital consisted of a medical resident, one or two interns, and three medical students. Our team's responsibility was to care for thirty to forty seriously ill people on our assigned ward. Every morning our team members gathered to evaluate our patients. At 7 a.m. the intern who cared for our established patients overnight and our new patients who were admitted into the hospital during the night gave his reports. Afterwards, the resident presented a didactic session to us about one of our new patient's illness and the treatment plan we would pursue. Thereafter, each member of the team received his patient assignments and duties for the morning. Our team reconvened about 11:30 a.m. to report to the resident in charge.

On my third day I was assigned a new patient named Oscar Wurner who not only had liver failure from alcoholism but also respiratory distress from chronic lung disease and a new pneumonia. My task for the morning was to obtain a comprehensive patient history from Oscar and to perform a thorough physical examination. (At least as thorough as I could do at the time.)

Oscar was a 48-year-old man who looked eighty to me. He smelled of alcohol and urine. I noticed that he was having some difficulty with breathing. However, he spoke with intelligence and seemed genuinely glad to talk with me.

My resident advised his medical students to talk with the patients and learn about them, not just their illnesses. So, instead of immediately asking Oscar about his breathing difficulties, I asked him, "Besides your breathing trouble, how have you been lately?"

With a puzzled look on his face, Oscar thought for a moment and said, "Nobody asked me that before. What do you care, anyway? I'm just a drunk."

I responded with, "I just want to learn a little bit about you if I could."

Oscar replied, "Well, okay. Where should I start?"

I told Oscar he could start anywhere he wanted.

He started his story on June 6, 1944, D-day. He was a twenty-year-old recruit in the army and in the second assault wave on Omaha Beach. Oscar described to me in detail how he saw his buddies get killed one after another. He told me that he should have died there too. Oscar told me that he was part of the force that liberated France. He was with the group that was under siege at Bastogne, Belgium, for seven days during the Battle of the Bulge. Oscar described for me briefly the atrocities he saw in the concentration camps in Germany. Oscar admitted that he wasn't right after the war. Oscar said he learned to drink and smoke in France. Oscar admitted that he drank and smoked cigarettes to excess. He could not keep a job. After several years, his wife divorced him and took away his child. He had not seen them for more than twenty years. Now he lived with other homeless veterans under the Burnside Bridge.

After taking Oscar's intriguing history, I performed a physical examination and recorded my findings on a notepad. Then I composed a detailed note for the chart.

At our late morning team meeting, I presented Oscar's case to the team for their assessments. After a discussion, the internal medicine resident proposed a treatment plan that I implemented that afternoon.

Part of the treatment plan required me to obtain a blood sample for a test called an arterial blood gas that would help us evaluate Oscar's lung function. The resident handed me an article titled, *"How to Perform an Arterial Puncture"* and told me not to come back without it.

Previously, I had obtained blood from a vein, but I had never seen, much less performed, an arterial puncture. After reading the article, I asked a nurse to collect the supplies that I needed: a glass syringe, some heparin (which was used to lubricate the inside of the syringe and to keep the blood from clotting), and the appropriately sized needle. The nurse placed the supplies onto a small metal tray and sent me on my way.

When I neared Oscar's bed in the ward, he just stared at me. I advised Oscar that I was asked to obtain a sample of blood from an artery in his wrist so we could evaluate how his lungs were performing. I asked his permission to perform the procedure.

Oscar continued to stare at me and said, "Young man, you don't have a clue what the heck you're going to do, do you?"

I replied, "I have never performed this procedure without supervision."

Oscar responded with, "Well, I'll be damned!" He thought for a moment and added, "I'll make you a deal."

"What kind of a deal?" I asked.

Oscar replied, "If you get me extra portions for my meals, I will not only let you get the blood, but I will show you how. What do you think about them apples?"

I agreed immediately.

Oscar said, "Okay, bring your stuff over here." He proceeded to show and tell me exactly what I had read in the article. When my syringe and needle were ready, Oscar told me to get a towel and roll it up. He placed the rolled towel under his left wrist with his palm facing upward. As he pointed toward his wrist, Oscar told me, "Put on some gloves."

After I had donned my examination gloves, he continued with, "Now feel my pulse right here. Clean it with alcohol. Draw the syringe barrel out about half an inch."

When I had completed these maneuvers, Oscar said, "Now stick the needle in at a thirty degree angle until the blood pumps up the syringe. You need to get about an inch worth of blood in the syringe."

When I looked at Oscar's wrist, I saw numerous small scabs from previous arterial punctures. I thought to myself, "This guy is an old pro at this, and a con artist to boot." With Oscar's help, I obtained the blood sample on my first try.

After the blood sample was obtained, Oscar reminded me to apply pressure on the artery for fifteen minutes by the clock so he wouldn't bleed to death.

I then took the blood to the lab for testing. The resident evaluated the results later that afternoon and determined a course of treatment for Oscar that I implemented.

I had the opportunity to obtain blood gas samples from Oscar several more times during his hospitalization. For the remainder of his stay in the hospital, I made sure that Oscar had extra food on his meal trays.

Oscar's pneumonia improved significantly over the next several weeks. He was discharged from the county hospital back to his home under the Burnside Bridge.

# MOST DAMP

During my first night on medicine call as a third-year medical student, I had the good fortune to meet, evaluate, and treat an amazing sixty-year-old man from Alberta, Canada, named Chadwick Churchill. Mr. Churchill fascinated me and our medical team for many reasons.

As a ten-year-old boy growing up on a farm near Calgary, Alberta, Canada, Mr. Churchill developed rheumatic fever in 1920 following a throat infection. (This was before penicillin was discovered.) Mr. Churchill gave me a textbook description of his disease and its progression. He recalled the rash, the joint pains, the profound weakness, and the year he spent bedridden.

Mr. Churchill described for me how he grew up to be a robust, physically fit farm boy. (At least that's what everyone thought.) With his business savvy and his farm profits, Mr. Churchill became an affluent man. He was able to perform all the physical duties on his farm until his early fifties when, *all of a sudden*, he could not. He fatigued easily. His strength waned rapidly over just a few months. A Canadian doctor in the late 1950s told Mr. Churchill that he had a heart murmur and an enlarged heart. The doctor informed Mr. Churchill that he had about a year to live. Mr. Churchill pointed out to us, however, that he had "no intention of rolling over and just kicking the bucket."

In the early 1960s, Mr. Churchill's heart was failing badly. He continued to look for medical solutions for his dilemma, both inside and outside of Canada.

In the late 1950s, a University of Oregon Medical School heart surgeon named Albert Starr and an Oregon engineer named Lowell Edwards invented the first implantable heart valve. Doctor Starr implanted the first successful heart valve replacement in Portland, Oregon, in 1960.

When Mr. Churchill discovered this achievement in the early 1960s, he tried to get the Canadian medical insurance system to pay for his heart care in the United States. When the Canadian government declined his request, Mr. Churchill paid his own way.

Despite having an enlarged, failing heart, Mr. Churchill had his faulty heart valve replaced. He told me something like, "They needed a guinea pig, and I needed a valve. There were no guarantees. They weren't sure the thing would work. I wasn't sure I would live long enough to see if it would work."

Sometime after his heart surgery, Mr. Churchill left Canada and moved to the Portland, Oregon area.

When our medical team visited with Mr. Churchill in the hospital, his heart was failing badly. Despite a new heart valve, which had extended his life about five years, Mr. Churchill knew his days were now numbered. However, he still was not willing to give up. That was not his way. He remained a fighter.

On this day, our team's examination of Mr. Churchill revealed rales in both lungs (a sound made in the lungs by air flowing through moisture), a massively enlarged heart, multiple loud heart murmurs, an enlarged liver (a sign of liver engorgement from heart failure), and profound leg swelling. When I pushed my finger into his water engorged leg tissues, a residual pit two centimeters deep remained. (This is called *pitting edema*.)

After our team's examination of Mr. Churchill, our medical resident discussed our patient's heart issues, the physiology of heart failure, and worked out a plan for my patient's care. The resident presented us with his phrase to remember the treatment of acute heart failure, MOST DAMP:

M = morphine (a medicine for pain and anxiety)
O = oxygen
S = sit up (to allow blood to pool in the legs and lung fluid to settle with gravity)
T = rotating tourniquets (to decrease blood flow to the heart)
D = digitalis (a medicine to increase the strength of heart contractions)
A = aminophylline (a medicine to open up lung airways)
M = mercurial diuretics (drugs that eliminate excess fluid through urination)
P = phlebotomy (a procedure to remove extra blood and fluid).
Doctors managing heart failure today have many more treatment options.

Mr. Churchill's heart failure worsened over the next few days despite our best efforts. Late one afternoon, he suffered a cardiac arrest. The nurse on duty called the medical resident on duty, the intern, and me to resuscitate Mr. Churchill. Our team used the MOST DAMP protocol that we had learned a few days before. We sat our patient upright in his bed and administered oxygen. I applied tourniquets to Mr. Churchill's right side extremities. After ten minutes, I reapplied them to his left side extremities. This process was continued for the duration of our resuscitation efforts. The intern administered morphine intravenously for sedation and pain relief. Also, the intern injected a new potent diuretic called Lasix that was more potent and predictable than the older mercurial diuretics. To facilitate our patient's urination, I was allowed to insert a bladder catheter, called a Foley catheter, which remained inside the bladder by way of an inflatable balloon. Mr. Churchill was already taking digitalis;[8] he needed no more from us because the medicine can be quite toxic if overdosed. Finally, the medical resident administered some aminophylline intravenously. He said, "This will make him better, or he'll die."

Our teamed tried to revive Mr. Churchill for almost two hours. He received electrical shocks and CPR.[9] We gave him every drug that we had to raise his blood pressure, but they didn't work. We tried every maneuver we could find in medicine's bedside bible, *The Washington Manual of Medical Therapeutics,* without success.

Mr. Churchill was my first patient to die.

---

[8] Digitalis is a medication that was originally derived from the foxglove plant (*Digitalis purpurea*) and used initially in the late eighteenth century to stimulate the heart when it was failing. One of the active chemicals derived during the digestion of the raw digitalis leaf is called digoxin. This chemical became the primary type of digitalis used because of its shorter duration of action and ease of production and standardization. Unfortunately, digitalis products have significant problems with toxicity. Digitalis use for heart failure was abandoned for the most during the late 1990s.

[9] CPR stands for cardiopulmonary resuscitation. It is a set of maneuvers including closed chest compressions and mouth-to-mouth breathing that are used to revive a person in shock. The American Heart Association establishes the guidelines for CPR.

# Gassed

I, like most medical students, never thought much about the potential consequences, both good and bad, regarding the things we did to our patients in the name of making them better. More precisely, we spent so much time memorizing science and ways to improve our patients' diseases that we students achieved little real life understanding of the bad things that *could* and *did* happen. All too often, our medical education involved what *could be done* to treat diseases while little time was spent on *what if* something didn't work or *what if* something goes wrong. In the minds of many students during our preclinical training, patients became faceless objects to be worked on by us the doctors. It became the patient's privilege to be seen by us.

In the spring of my third year in medical school, I had a pediatric rotation for eight weeks at a private hospital in north Portland. I had spent much of my spare time during the previous two years observing in the obstetrics department at the Multnomah County Hospital and in the medical school's pediatric intensive care unit. I became reasonably comfortable with the observation and evaluation of healthy, normal newborns as well as sick, premature infants. On a few occasions, I witnessed how a normal newborn infant *went sour* and died for no good reason that the doctors could determine. I saw how sick, premature infants before 36 weeks gestation usually died because of lung immaturity or infections. The pediatricians at the time were helpless because they had few therapeutic tools to help these children. At the beginning of my pediatrics rotation, I was far more experienced in pediatrics than many of my classmates who had little or no prior medical experience caring for children.

One of our *extras* on pediatrics was being able to assist the local pediatric surgeon during surgery, if we wanted. Fortunately for me, I was the only student on my team who was interested in surgery. Therefore, I had the opportunity to assist caring for children with burns, both before and after surgery. I evaluated children with cleft lips and palates and other congenital abnormalities before they underwent reconstructive surgery. Not once did I witness an unforeseen outcome. I was lured into believing that most things doctors did was magical and without complications.

In my era before outpatient surgery, surgical patients came to the hospital the night before their scheduled procedure. The patient was evaluated that evening and pre-surgical orders were written. The same rules applied to children. The child's parents usually spent the night in a hospital bed next to their child.

One evening, I had the opportunity to evaluate a six-year-old child, who I will name Johnny. Johnny, a patient of Doctor Carson, the pediatric surgeon, was scheduled to have an elective inguinal hernia repair the next morning. After my evaluation of Johnny, I called Doctor Carson to tell him that his patient was not ill and appeared to have a massive inguinal hernia[10] on the left side. I told him that Johnny should be okay for surgery the next morning.

Doctor Carson asked me to first mark the hernia site with an indelible marker and then to call the anesthesiologist (the doctor who administers the anesthesia) for the case so he too could evaluate Johnny and confirm my evaluation.

The anesthesiologist and I visited Johnny and talked with his mom that evening. He confirmed my evaluation and then called the surgeon. He told Doctor Carson that, "All was a go for seven bells."

A few minutes before 7 o'clock the next morning, Doctor Carson and I dressed in surgical garb and applied special cloth shoe covers with an electrical grounding strip on them that helped reduce static electricity in the operating room. We scrubbed our hands and prepared to perform surgery. Before we entered the surgical suite, we walked on a damp towel.

I asked why there was a wet towel on the floor.

An operating room nurse informed me that the anesthetic gas, cyclopropane or cyclo, could be flammable. The towel wet our shoes to help eliminate any static electricity.

Doctor Carson started the operation. He talked all the time as he explained to me exactly how he repaired hernias in children. Doctor Carson even let me tie a few knots – quite a thrill for a medical student.

As Doctor Carson was preparing to close the skin wound, we heard a low-tone *"pop"* sound.

---

[10] An inguinal hernia is a defect in the lower abdominal wall that occurs in up to 25 percent of males and 3 percent of females. The abnormality presents as a bulge in the lower abdomen that is caused by abdominal contents being forced through the anatomical defect in the layers of the abdominal wall. Hernia repair is one of the most common surgical procedures.

The anesthesiologist grunted, "Damn!"

Doctor Carson asked, "Any problem up there?"

The anesthesiologist replied calmly, "Your patient is dead. His lungs just blew up from a spark in the gas."

In disbelief, Doctor Carson responded, "Are you sure?"

The stunned anesthesiologist replied, "Yes, I'm sure! There was a spark in the tubing, and the kid's lungs exploded! Trust me, he's dead!" After a few moments, he muttered, "I'd better call my insurance company."

Doctor Carson felt for pulses but found none. He looked at the heart monitor to see only a flat line. This meant that there was no heart activity. I could see him close his eyes and point his face toward the ceiling, but he didn't say a word. His surgical mask became wet with his tears. After a few moments of reflection, Doctor Carson looked at me and said, "Doctor Ashcraft, we have an operation to finish, don't we? Let's get to it."

I didn't say a word. I just nodded in approval.

Doctor Carson allowed me to close the skin over the hernia repair.

When I was finished, the anesthesiologist said, "I'm sorry gentlemen, but I need a moment alone. Then, I'll talk with the parents." He stood up and walked out of the operating room.

Doctor Carson removed the surgical drapes and picked up the dead boy. He hugged his patient, and said quietly, "Johnny, I am so sorry. I am so sorry." He then asked the surgical nurses to make Johnny presentable for his mom and to cancel his remaining cases for the day.

Doctor Carson and I didn't talk while we dressed. I did not know what to say. This was my first experience with a *real* complication. I remember thinking, "Johnny was *my* patient, and he died because of an *adverse event.*" He became just another statistic for the academics, but to his mom, the anesthesiologist, Doctor Carson, and to me, Johnny's death was a personal tragedy. I knew Johnny trusted his doctors, and we had let him down. Our medicine killed him because of an *adverse event.*

After we were dressed, Doctor Carson looked at me and said, "Jim, most of the time, medicine is fun beyond belief. Sometimes shit happens." After a short pause to reflect, he said, "The way you feel now will pass, but the memories will stay. I believe that's a good thing. Those memories will make you a better physician."

As we were walking down the hospital corridor, Doctor Carson said, "You go ahead and catch up with your team. I have to talk with Johnny's mom. I'll be a while.... quite a while."

Years later, when I arrived in Sidney, Montana, the anesthetic gas used in surgery was *cyclopropane*.

I remembered Johnny.

When safer anesthetics became available, cyclopropane was banned from our hospital.

# VA Surgery

I spent the summer of my fourth year in medical school learning surgery at the Veterans Hospital (the VA) in Portland, Oregon. Unlike today's new, modern facility, the VA that I knew was an aging, deteriorating facility awaiting demolition. Nonetheless, it housed some of the latest technology of the day including radiology facilities to perform cardiac catheterization with angiograms (special x-rays of blood vessels), open-heart surgery operating rooms, and modern intensive care units.

Including me, our VA surgical team had five members:

1. Donald Slocum was the chief resident surgeon who aspired to be a plastic surgeon.
2. Myron George, a family medicine resident who had just returned from serving three years in the Public Health Service on an isolated island off the Alaska coast, was retooling before he entered private practice.
3. Henry Walter was a first-year ear, nose, and throat (ENT) surgery resident.
4. Tom Harkins was a fellow fourth-year medical student.

Often, our duties with our surgical patients did not coincide with mealtimes at the VA. Therefore, the cafeteria staff allowed us to have a key for after hours dining. This key was affectionately called *The Cheese Key*. I soon learned that the cafeteria, or as the veterans called it, The Canteen, concocted some interesting dishes, including peanut butter soup, liver with Brussels sprouts, and liver and avocado sandwiches. The cheese key gained us entry to the cafeteria after hours to enjoy what was left of the gourmet delight for that day. Since most of the food had been sitting out in the open air for hours before our arrival, we usually ended up eating dried cheese with bread (hence the name cheese key).

Along with our regular hospital duties, our mandatory assignment during our surgery rotation at the VA was to read and outline the fifteen hundred pages of the surgical textbook, *Schwartz's Principles of Surgery*. Apparently, the chief of surgery at the VA didn't want his medical students to have any down time.

It did not take me long to figure out that the other members of our team had substantially different levels of medical training. Also, they had different degrees of interest in learning about and performing general surgery. For example, there was the case of the elderly veteran with a bowel obstruction.

Doctor Slocum and I were in the operating room removing a patient's ruptured appendix one evening when Doctor George, who was evaluating patients in the emergency room, called. Doctor George informed Doctor Slocum that he had a man in the emergency room with a bowel obstruction who was throwing up material that looked like feces. Doctor George told us that he thought the man needed an operation pronto.

Doctor Slocum asked, "Myron, is the guy stable?"

To this, Doctor George replied, "Don, he's stable like a rock."

Doctor Slocum returned with, "Okay, Myron, make sure he has plenty of fluids. Make sure his blood test results are good. Then, send him up to pre-op. I'll work on him as soon as Jim and I finish with this guy's rotten appendix."

In the early hours of the morning, we completed the appendectomy. Doctor Slocum was hungry, so we grabbed the cheese key and headed toward The Canteen to get some food.

The offerings this night included some dried up tuna (tuna jerky), several slices of dried liver (liver jerky), shriveled cheese slices (cheese jerky), some dry, stale bread (a.k.a. shingles), and orange juice. After looking over our food choices, Doctor Slocum and I decided that we weren't as hungry as we thought and elected to drink the orange juice.

Upon our return to the operating room, our patient from the emergency room was being readied for surgery by the anesthesiologist. When our patient was asleep, the anesthesiologist told Doctor Slocum, "Don, He's ready for you."

After cleaning the man's abdomen with soap and applying sterile drapes over our patient, Doctor Slocum made an incision to begin the operation.

The anesthesiologist called out promptly, "Don, hold on a minute. Our man's got some trouble with his blood pressure. Give me a few minutes to get in some fluids."

Doctor Slocum asked, "What is his BP? (blood pressure)

The anesthesiologist replied, "It was 110 over 70 (110/70) when he came in. Now, it's 60" (normal is about 120/80 standing or lying down).

After a few minutes of waiting and the patient's blood pressure still had not improved substantially, Doctor Slocum asked the surgical nurse supervisor to contact Doctor George in the emergency room.

Soon, the nurse transferred Doctor George's call to the operating room's intercom. Doctor George asked, "Hey Don, what's up?"

To this Doctor Slocum said, "Myron, we're having some blood pressure troubles with the guy you sent up with a bowel obstruction. I thought you said he was stable as a rock?"

Doctor George replied, "He was."

Doctor Slocum countered with, "What was his BP in the ER?"

To this Doctor George said, "I'm looking at the chart. It was 110 over 70."

Doctor Slocum asked, "What was it when he stood up?"

Doctor George replied, "Couldn't take it standing. *He kept passing out.*"

With this, Doctor Slocum looked up at the ceiling, looked at me, looked at the anesthesiologist, and then said, "Myron, that means the guy was in shock. That's a pretty important thing for us to know *before* we put a patient to sleep. Myron, we need to talk later."

Doctor Slocum expressed his apologies to the anesthesiologist for the trouble he had caused. (He took the blame for Myron.) He told the anesthesiologist to take as much time as he needed to get the patient stable.

When our patient was fully hydrated with intravenous fluids and his blood pressure normalized, Doctor Slocum and I continued with the operation. Doctor Slocum removed a cancer that had obstructed the man's colon and diverted the intestine to the outside of the abdomen. I was allowed to suture the other end of the colon shut. Doctor Slocum also allowed me to close the abdominal wound before he attached a colostomy bag to the man's abdomen.

That night, Doctor Slocum decided that Doctor George had forgotten much of his medical training during his time in isolation in Alaska. As a consequence, Doctor George was assigned to a remedial curriculum of experiences to prepare him to enter private practice after a year. This meant that Doctor George spent considerable time evaluating and stabilizing patients in the emergency room and not in the operating room.

Doctor Walter wanted to spend most of his time upstairs on the ENT floor. This was fine with Doctor Slocum, because he didn't want people around him who weren't interested in doing general surgery. Except being present for our twice-daily hospital rounds, Doctor Walter became our team's *surgeon in absentia*.

Tom Harkins was not exactly enthusiastic about his surgery rotation either. However, he did do what was asked of him, but not much more.

I, however, was like a kid in a candy store. I truly enjoyed learning about surgery, performing surgery, and caring for post-surgical patients. I did not mind spending the entire day performing surgery, even though the student rotation manual forbid this activity. The VA was chronically understaffed, and the residents always appreciated an extra pair of hands. Overtime duty by medical students was rarely reported.

Doctor Slocum and I soon became friends. It seemed that we operated together most days, and nights. He showed me how to fix hernias, repair intestines, open and drain abscesses, apply skin grafts, remove gallbladders and appendices, and successfully perform many other procedures.

One morning near the end of my surgical rotation, Doctor Slocum sent me to the nearby orthopedics surgical suite where the senior orthopedic resident told me, "Don Slocum said you're a good hand."

I figured I was going to assist the orthopedic resident with his surgery. To my surprise and delight, the orthopedist allowed me to perform his surgery. With the orthopedist's supervision and instructions, I repaired a fractured hip.

Some years later, Doctor Slocum joined a plastic surgery practice in Billings, Montana. I renewed our friendship and referred patients to him for a few years. Unfortunately, he was diagnosed with malignant melanoma that was quite aggressive. Despite heroic efforts to kill the tumor, including a bone marrow transplant, Doctor Slocum died a short time after his diagnosis was made.

# A Tune-up

Harvey Whitaker was a widower in his mid-seventies. I first met him during the summer when I was on my surgical rotation at the Portland Veterans Hospital (VA). He was one of my first surgical patients as a fourth-year medical student. Harvey proudly informed me that he was "just one of General Pershing's doughboys" in World War I. Harvey told me that he was admitted to the hospital from the emergency room for a repair of his groin hernia that was located in his lower abdomen.

Apparently, Harvey's hernia had become trapped in the layers of his abdominal wall (called incarcerated) the day before while he was moving stuff around his home. The stuck hernia produced severe pain that kept him awake all that night. The next morning, Harvey came to the VA emergency room. The physician on duty released the obstruction, and told Harvey that the hernia had to be repaired "right away." Taking the doctor's advice, Harvey entered the hospital to have his hernia fixed "right away." (In the 1960s and 1970s, it was not uncommon for a veteran to spend a week or two in the hospital before an elective surgery was performed.)

The hernia's incarceration and subsequent reduction maneuvers produced considerable bruising and swelling of the surrounding soft tissues. After allowing several days for the swelling to subside, our chief surgical resident, Doctor Donald Slocum, and I took Harvey to the operating room where Doctor Slocum repaired the hernia defect. I was allowed to close the entire wound after the repair was completed.

At the time, the usual recovery stay in the VA after a hernia repair was about two weeks. (Now, with same-day surgery, it's a few hours.) Since his surgery was not complicated, I anticipated that Harvey would settle in for a routine two-week post-op vacation at the VA.

One afternoon, after Harvey had been in the hospital about a week, a nurse summoned me. The nurse told me that my patient was having severe abdominal pain after eating lunch. She thought Harvey needed to be evaluated now.

When I questioned the nurse about whether or not my patient had other symptoms besides pain, such as nausea, vomiting, fever, chills, etc., she curtly answered, "No."

I then made my way to Harvey's room. I found Harvey lying still in his bed with both hands over his upper abdomen. I noticed his partially consumed lunch at his bedside. I thought to myself, "Maybe he has food poisoning. The VA food really was not that great."

When I asked Harvey to tell me what happened, he told me that he got a really bad bellyache while eating a polish hotdog with sauerkraut. He said the pain went into his back on the right side and into his right shoulder. However, the pain was a little better if he pressed hard on his belly.

When questioned, Harvey denied ever having pain like this before.

My examination revealed acute tenderness in the right upper quadrant of Harvey's abdomen. The pain seemed most intense right under his rib cage. Harvey told me that the back and shoulder pains returned when I pushed on his belly. I knew he was having an acute gallbladder attack.

I telephoned Doctor Slocum to advise him of my findings and my preliminary diagnosis. After a short consultation, Doctor Slocum asked me to order an oral cholecystogram for the next morning. (This is an x-ray using a special contrast dye. This was the usual test for gallbladder disease at the time. Today, this test has been replaced, for the most part, by ultrasounds or CAT scans.)

Harvey had the x-ray. It revealed a gallbladder full of stones.

Doctor Slocum advised Harvey, "Your gallbladder has to come out *before* you leave the hospital."

Harvey just replied, "Whatever you say, Doc."

I scheduled Harvey for gallbladder surgery to be done one week later.

A few days later, I was on weekend duty with Doctor Slocum. On rounds in the morning, Harvey complained to us that he was having some pressure in his chest. He felt short of breath too. When I asked him if the discomfort went anywhere, Harvey said, "Yeah, Doc, it goes down my left arm all the way to my pinky finger."

Promptly, I summoned a nurse to bring a nitroglycerin pill for my patient. She placed one tablet under Harvey's tongue. While the nitroglycerin was working, I performed an electrocardiogram (a heart activity tracing or ECG). I noticed that the ECG revealed a pattern consistent with acute ischemia or injury.

Doctor Slocum asked me, "How did you read that so fast? It takes me at least ten minutes every time I read one."

I replied, "I worked as a tech in the cardiac ICU last year."

The ECG machine was still attached to Harvey and running when the nitroglycerin took effect. We watched the ECG tracing as the injury pattern resolved. However, Doctor Slocum and I knew that Harvey had a significant heart issue. Harvey's gallbladder surgery would have to be postponed until his heart problem was corrected.

Doctor Slocum called the cardiology resident on duty. Within minutes, Harvey was whisked away to cardiology.

My surgery rotation ended about a month later. I left for my next rotation without having an opportunity to visit with Harvey again.

In the fall several months later, I, along with several other fourth-year students, had a neurology rotation at the VA. While making morning rounds on my first day, the neurology resident gave each of us several patients to evaluate. One of my patients was Harvey Whitaker.

According to the neurology resident, Mr. Whitaker's had a TIA (transient ischemia attack or pre-stroke) after surgery. The surgeons wanted him evaluated by neurology before going home.

Since I knew more of Harvey's history, I figured that he finally got his gallbladder removed after his heart problem was rectified. When I asked Mr. Whitaker when he got his gallbladder taken out, he quipped, "Haven't."

I asked Harvey what happened after the heart doctors took him from the surgery floor.

Harvey told me the heart doctors took him straight in to have a dye test on his heart (an angiogram). They found a blockage in two of the arteries to the heart. They also found a blockage in Harvey's neck artery (the carotid artery) on the left side.

I asked him what happened next.

Harvey said that his heart doctors called in two heart surgeons. They couldn't decide if they should fix his heart or his neck first. He thought the two doctors finally just drew straws. The heart surgery won out. Soon, they bypassed Harvey's heart. He was getting along just fine afterward except for chest pain where they cut his breastbone. Harvey thought for a few moments. Then he told me that after a while he got bored. He wanted to go home, but the heart surgeons observed him acting "funny" one morning and informed Harvey it was time to have neck surgery. The next day the surgeons repaired the blockage in his neck.

I asked if everything had gone as planned.

Harvey thought so, as far as he knew. The surgeons checked him everyday for almost a month. The day before he came to neurology, a nurse told the doctors that he was "acting goofy again." Thus, Harvey was transferred to neurology for an assessment before he could go home.

After this discussion, I completed a mental status examination for Harvey that was unremarkable for someone in his mid-seventies. My examination revealed recent surgical scars on Harvey's chest, left neck, and left lower abdomen (from his hernia repair months before). I noticed slight weakness in his *left* hand grip and his *left* arm. (These findings correlate to a defect on the *right side* of the brain. The carotid surgery he underwent had protected the *left side* of the brain.)

When I discussed my findings with the neurology resident, he told me that he noticed the same neurological deficits. The resident thought that Harvey needed to be observed and evaluated a little longer in neurology.

Harvey Whitaker was still a patient on the VA neurology ward when I departed for my next rotation.

The following February, I started my two-week rotation in urology at the VA. The chief resident was a quiet, red-haired physician named Ned Skooters. Doctor Skooters was nearing the end of his four-year residency in urology and was making plans to enter private practice in southern Oregon in a few months.

Soon after my arrival, Doctor Skooters asked me to perform a consultation on an elderly surgical patient who was having trouble urinating. Doctor Skooters did not know the patient's name, but he had the man's room number on the VA general surgery wing. I was given instructions to evaluate the patient and to call Doctor Skooters before I returned to urology.

I made my way to the general surgery wing. I looked up the chart for the room number I had been given, and, to my surprise, it was the chart for Harvey Whitaker. While reviewing his chart I noticed it had a considerable amount of history missing. Additionally, I noticed that Mr. Whitaker finally had his gallbladder removed just a few days before.

When I walked into Mr. Whitaker's room, his eyes lit up when he saw me. He said, "Well, aren't you a sight for sore eyes?"

When I asked him how he had been, Harvey replied, "Since when?"

I answered, "Well, how about since I last saw you on neurology?"

Harvey told me that the neurologist did another dye test on his neck and found a blockage on the right side. The left side, of course, was wide-open from the recent surgery. Harvey continued to tell me that he had another operation to fix a right carotid artery blockage.

I asked Harvey how he got to general surgery.

He explained that one day while he was recuperating from his second neck surgery, his belly pains returned. Somebody noticed in the chart that he had a gallbladder attack a few months before and was scheduled to have his gallbladder removed. Harvey said, "Well, you know how the VA works. One thing leads to another. One doctor talks to another doctor...." After thinking for a few moments, Harvey continued, "The surgeon I have now said I couldn't leave this place with my gallbladder. I think that's what somebody told me months ago. Anyway, he took out my gallbladder two days ago. Now, I can't pee." Pointing to a catheter coming out the end of his penis, Harvey exclaimed, "See, they put a drain tube in my me."

Harvey's explanation was so animated I almost laughed. However, I knew that an acute urinary obstruction was no laughing matter.

I continued to complete another history and physical examination for Mr. Whitaker. I noticed that his left-side weakness had resolved and there were recent scars on the left side of his neck and his right upper abdomen.

After I finished writing my detailed history and physical examination in Mr. Whitaker's chart, I called Doctor Skooters. When I told him about Harvey Whitaker's months-long adventure inside the Portland Veterans Hospital, there was silence on the telephone. Then I heard Doctor Skooters laughing out loud. When he returned to the telephone, Doctor Skooters exclaimed, "Ashcraft, are you kidding me?"

When I assured him that I was not telling a joke, Doctor Skooters said, "I gotta see this guy! I'll be right there."

Within a few minutes, my resident physician was reviewing my history and physical examination. When Doctor Skooters finished reading Harvey's chart, we went to see Mr. Whitaker.

As I entered the room with Doctor Skooters, Mr. Whitaker looked at me and asked, "Now, what's this guy going to do to me?"

I introduced Harvey to Doctor Skooters who stated, "Hello, sir. I'm Doctor Skooters. I have been discussing your situation with Doctor Ashcraft. I must admit, you two have had quite a journey the past six months."

Harvey responded with, "Boy, you're telling me!"

After his examination of Harvey's prostate, Doctor Skooters said, "Partner, your prostate is too big. It's plugging up your pee channel. I think I can help you." Doctor Skooters then went on to explain to Harvey what he would need to do to his prostate gland.

Harvey said he couldn't go home like an elephant. He told Doctor Skooters to do what he had to do.

Doctor Skooters agreed to make the arrangements for Harvey's surgery as soon as possible.

As we were leaving his room, Harvey called out to us and motioned with his hand for us to return. When we were back at the bedside, Harvey said, "Gentlemen, did you see my unit down there? I've wanted to have it circumcised since World War I. Since I've been here at the VA, I've had a hernia fixed, my heart bypassed, my neck arteries opened twice, my gallbladder taken out, and now my prostate is going to be Roto-Rootered. How about fixing my unit while you're down there?"

Doctor Skooters smiled and said, "Consider it done."

Before we exited the room, Harvey remarked, "When my neighbors ask me where I've been, I can tell them I had a complete VA tune-up!"

A few days later, Harvey Whitaker was taken to the operating room to have part of his prostate gland removed by Doctor Skooters. After the prostate surgery was completed, I had the privilege of performing Harvey's circumcision, the crowning touch to his *Complete VA Tune-up.*

Harvey Whitaker finally left the Portland Veterans Hospital several weeks later.

# More to Learn

Given one well-trained physician of the highest type he will do better work for a thousand people than ten specialists.

William J. Mayo, M.D.

# Welcome to Pediatrics

The first day, the entire group of interns met with the hospital's medical director and his staff who gave us a full day of orientation to the twelve-story Sacred Heart Hospital complex in Spokane, Washington. Each intern was assigned a room in a building across the street from the hospital where we could rest (when and if he had time) or live full time if he wished. (Interns were still interned at the facility.) We learned about meals in the cafeteria and where snacks were located throughout the hospital. (Obstetrics had the biggest stash of goodies.) We learned about the strict dress code of a white doctor's jacket and a tie. Wearing surgical scrub suits was acceptable when on-call or on a surgical rotation. Each of us received a pager so we would not miss anything.

The second day was filled with classes on how to resuscitate a patient (CPR) and how to use the drugs and equipment during a cardiac arrest event (a CODE). We had a class on the basics of suturing wounds and applying casts. Compared to today, this was a minimal introduction to the internship. Initial orientation for new graduates now requires a week or longer and includes classes in Basic CPR, ACLS (Advanced Cardiac Life Support), PALS (Pediatric Advanced Life Support), NALS (Newborn Advanced Life Support), and finally, ALSO (Advanced Life Support Obstetrics). Talk about alphabet soup!

The third day produced orientations to the medical records department and the hospital's dictation system, to the clinical laboratory, and to the medical library. The last session of the day included a group question and answer discussion to uncover any last minute dilemmas. The medical director's secretary handed out our clinical rotation assignments for the year and the first on-call schedule. My first eight-weeks rotation was pediatrics. When on call my assignment was to cover nighttime emergencies for pediatrics, surgery, and psychiatry on floors two, four, and twelve. I was in a panic before I even started.

The next morning I rode my bike from our home about five miles to the hospital. I arrived early enough to shower in my new intern quarters before I went to the pediatrics floor. I arrived on the pediatrics floor about 7 a.m. attired with my new white coat and tie and my little black bag. I had my *peripheral brains*, a small notebook and the interns' pediatric bible, the <u>Harriet Lane Manual of Pediatrics</u>, in my coat pocket. I introduced myself as Doctor Ashcraft to a nurse on duty who directed me to speak to her head nurse. The nurse advised me of the times when the various pediatricians with whom I would be working usually arrived to make their morning patient visits (rounds).

About a half hour later, another intern named Red Roberts arrived. We were paired for eight weeks on the pediatrics floor. Red made it clear early on that he really did not like kids; he wanted to be a surgeon; he had accepted a surgical residency position that started in a year; he felt he was just putting in his time at Sacred Heart.

I thought to myself, "I like pediatrics, and I'm ready to get going!"

The nurse advised us that the pediatrics ward had about forty sick kids with a severe upper respiratory disease, croup, asthma, or influenza, or gastroenteritis (vomiting and diarrhea) with dehydration. She advised us to, "Wash your hands before *and* after examining patients." She suggested that we might want to carry some diapers with us *just in case.*

Our first preceptor, Doctor Kendrick Staffen, arrived just after 8 a.m. He and his partner, Doctor Vincent Capra, had a busy pediatrics practice that operated out of two offices in the Spokane area. Doctor Ken, as he liked to be called, had just come from the hospital emergency room where he had evaluated and admitted an eight-month-old boy with gastroenteritis. Doctor Ken requested that either Doctor Roberts or I evaluate his patient after the boy and his mother arrived on the pediatrics ward. Doctor Ken asked that we telephone him later to discuss a plan of treatment. He had already written some admission orders in the emergency room. Red and I flipped coins; I won the toss.

Red and I completed rounds with Doctor Ken that morning. The new patient arrived about the time Doctor Staffen was ready to leave. Doctor Staffen introduced the child's mother to me, told her of his plan for her baby's care, and asked the mother to call me if she had any questions about her child. Doctor Ken then exited for his office.

The mother left for home to clean up after the nurse reassured her that her child would be well cared for by the hospital staff. She related that she would be back soon, but before she left, made sure that we had her telephone number to call if any problems arose before she returned.

Doctor Ken assigned Doctor Roberts and me several patients to evaluate that morning. While Red went off to see his assigned children, the head nurse and I went to evaluate the new admission, a baby boy with gastroenteritis.[11]

My first impression of the child while looking at him was that he was not very ill. He was playful, had a wet mouth, and did not appear to me to be dehydrated. I mentioned my thoughts to the nurse who informed me that Doctor Ken usually has a good reason for admitting his kids.

I decided to weigh and measure the baby to obtain some baseline data. I asked the nurse to prepare a nearby baby scale with a clean paper liner so I could weigh the baby. After the liner had been applied, I undressed the little boy. I took his temperature with a rectal thermometer. It read 103 degrees. I picked the patient up by his armpits to hold him upright (to assess the muscle control of his head and neck). As I held the little boy in the air facing me, he, in rapid succession, vomited on my new white coat and my face, urinated on my tie and shirt, and let loose a runny yellow stool that went down the front of my pants and landed on my shoes.

I must have looked shocked. I was a smelly mess!

The nurse giggled. Showing a big smile she proclaimed, "Doctor Ashcraft, welcome to pediatrics."

Later that day on evening rounds, I asked Doctor Ken why he had admitted the child. I mentioned that the baby did not appear very ill.

He told me that the mom had three other kids at home, and he thought she needed a break.

---

[11] Gastroenteritis is a nonspecific term for an inflammation of the stomach and the intestines. In children, the disorder is common and is usually caused by a viral infection. The disorder usually resolves spontaneously if fluids are administered judiciously.

# Call Night

During my internship each intern was on call at night for their selected areas every three days, except obstetrics. This rotation required being on the OB floor for 24 hours every two days. (With the usual workload to be done during the days, the obstetrics rotation required our availability 36 out of every 48 hours.) Night call started at 5 p.m. and ended at 6 a.m. the following day.

My first night on call was scheduled for the third day of my internship. I was glad for this because I was anxious about how I would perform. The two extra days gave me time to ask the other interns about their on-call experiences. One of the interns informed me that he slept most of his first night on call. When I learned that they all survived without any major catastrophes, I knew I was ready.

My first assignment as an intern was on the pediatrics service of the hospital. However, this was a rotating internship. Our training was aimed at teaching us multiple disciplines at the same time. Therefore, when on night call, the pediatrics interns were expected to be available for in-house emergencies not only for pediatrics but also for surgery and psychiatry. Surgery was on the second floor, pediatrics occupied the fourth floor, and psychiatry filled the twelfth floor.

My pager started to ring at 5:04 p.m. The first call was from the surgical intensive care unit. A seventy-year-old man who had undergone a stomach surgery that morning was vomiting blood. The nurse could not find the surgeon on call. She needed me now (STAT)!

As I made my way down the stairs to surgery on the second floor, my pager went off again. It was now 5:07 p.m. The nurse in psychiatry on the twelfth floor told me that a male patient had pulled out his radial artery from his wrist with a plastic fork. Blood was everywhere! She too wanted me STAT! I told her I was headed to the surgical ICU. I asked her to put a compression bandage on the wrist with an elastic wrap and gauze. I would be there when I could.

Just as I walked into the surgical ICU, my pager went off again. It was now 5:09 p.m. A nurse in the emergency room told me that she had just transferred a six-year-old child having a severe asthma attack to the pediatrics floor. The child should be there soon. The ER nurse ordered me there STAT!

I had three pending catastrophes within ten minutes. I nearly panicked, but after I took a few deep breaths and recalled the ABC priorities (airway, breathing, circulation), I was anxious but in control of my emotions.

By the time I attended the surgery patient, his vomiting of blood had mostly subsided. However, I estimated that he had lost about 2000 milliliters of blood (about two quarts). His vital signs were awful after losing so much blood. I inserted another large bore intravenous line for more fluids and blood. I asked the nurse to have the lab type and cross match six units of whole blood[12] STAT! I asked her to give our patient four units of blood when they arrived. If our patient started to bleed again before the cross-matched blood was ready, I told the nurse to rapidly give two units of blood with the same blood type but without spending time to cross match the blood. (There were no worries with AIDS or Hepatitis C infections in those days.)

While attending to the surgery patient, I asked the ward clerk to check on my other two patients. The young ward clerk soon advised me that the man in psychiatry was combative and crazy. The psychiatry nurse needed something to calm him down now. The pediatric nurse said the asthmatic child was holding her own.

I called psychiatry and told the nurse to give our crazy man two milliliters of Inapsine in his butt every fifteen minutes until he collapsed. (Inapsine is a rapidly acting antipsychotic with few cardiac or respiratory side effects that worked well with agitated patients.) I asked the psychiatry nurse to keep me updated on the patient. She noted that the pressure bandage had been applied, the bleeding had stopped, and the man was in full restraints.

The surgical patient's vital signs stabilized after a copious amount of intravenous saline. I reminded the nurse to give the blood when it arrived. Since this patient was now relatively stable, I told the ICU nurse that I was headed upstairs to pediatrics.

---

[12] Whole blood contains all the elements of blood. In my training days, whole blood was used as the total volume replacement product. Today, the blood is separated into its components. Today, whole blood has been replaced by packed red cells, which is whole blood minus the fluid components.

She could call me if I was needed. I then ran up the stairs to pediatrics.

Upon entering the child's room, I could see that the little girl was having difficulty breathing. Listening with my stethoscope, I heard essentially no air movement in the child's lungs. Her lips were blue. Her neck veins were distended as she strained to breathe. I quickly looked at the medications she had already received: oxygen, oral aminophylline, intramuscular epinephrine, and albuterol by an aerosol. No blood gases or other lab tests had been done to evaluate how the lungs were working. The child did have an intravenous catheter in place. I recalled being in a similar situation during my medical school experiences on the pediatrics floor at Emmanuel Hospital in Portland, Oregon.

I asked what the child weighed. When I received the answer, I ordered .015 milliliters per kilogram of Susphrine (a long-acting epinephrine) to be given subcutaneously now and every two hours as long as the child was experiencing respiratory trouble. I had the nurse give the aerosol in a continuous mist instead of every three hours as it was originally ordered. When all of these maneuvers had been completed, I asked that the lab be called to obtain blood for testing.

Within a few minutes the child's breathing improved enough so that I could now hear some air movement with wheezing. I knew then that my treatment was on the right track.

About now the child's mother said her child got into something to which she had allergies. I figured that this asthma episode could be mostly caused by an acute allergy. Therefore, I administered an antihistamine by injection, which I hoped would quiet down any allergy symptoms and sedate the child at the same time. (Today we would give cortisone. However, at this time, most pediatricians frowned upon the use of cortisone for asthma in children.)

I remained with the child for about two hours before I called the family's pediatrician, Doctor Vincent Capra. I informed him of his patient's improved status, what I had done, and that I would call him hourly if he wished.

Doctor Capra said it sounded like I had everything under control. He asked me to call him if I had questions or if the child's condition worsened.

The surgical nurse had been keeping me updated on our patient. He had no more active bleeding, the blood was infusing, the vital signs were stable, and the surgeon had been located. Apparently, he had failed to charge his pager.

I paged the surgeon. He told me that he had seen our patient. He agreed with what I had done, and he resumed caring for his patient. He thanked me for my efforts.

It was almost 8 p.m. when I finally made it to psychiatry on the twelfth floor. The nurse took me to our patient who had required three injections of Inapsine to put him to sleep. While the man snored, I removed the bandage from his wrist, evaluated the pulsating radial artery that was protruding from a gash in the skin, and placed a single ligature on the blood vessel just in case something else happened. After I evaluated the circulation to the man's hand and found it to be satisfactory, I called the vascular surgeon on-call for the hospital. After I related the situation to him, the surgeon decided that the arm could be re-bandaged for the evening. He planned to evaluate the man in the morning. He asked that I keep the man sedated for the rest of the evening, if possible.

I left orders for medications that I hoped would keep the man sedated. Before I left psychiatry for pediatrics, I thanked the psychiatric nurse for her help. I asked her to page me if she had any problems. Thankfully, I did not hear from anyone in psychiatry the rest of this night.

Returning to the bedside of my little girl with asthma, I noticed that she had fallen asleep and her color had improved. Her pulse was about 140 from the medications. Her respiratory rate had dropped from about sixty to about thirty. I could hear much better air movement in her lungs and no wheezes. I looked at the nurse attending the child. She smiled as if to say, "We did good!"

I whispered, "So far, so good. Let's keep our fingers crossed."

Just as I was considering lying down to take a short rest, I received a page from the surgical ICU. The nurse told me our patient was having trouble breathing. His surgeon was performing an emergency operation and had asked if I could see his patient. Off I went downstairs to the ICU.

Our patient indeed was short of breath. He was gasping for air. I looked at his fluid intake and output record. His intravenous fluid intake was far greater than his urinary output. I could hear little air movement in his lungs. I knew that we had put the man into heart failure. A dose of intravenous diuretics should resolve this problem, I thought.

While the nurse readied the dose of diuretic medication, I asked the radiology department to perform a chest x-ray on my patient. In a short time, I had a chest x-ray that revealed not only fluid in the lungs from heart failure but also evidence for emphysema with a collapsed left lung.

While the ICU nurse obtained the instruments for a chest tube insertion and the materials for a suction and drainage apparatus, I called the operating room to give the surgeon an update. I asked his permission to insert a chest tube into his patient. After I told him how I would perform the procedure, he gave me permission. The surgeon reminded me to insert the needle on top of the rib because the blood vessels are on the bottom of the rib. He reminded me that I had been an intern for only three days.

The nurse and I inserted the chest tube without incident. I had done this procedure several times before as a medical student. A repeat x-ray revealed that the left lung had re-inflated. The man was urinating like a racehorse from the diuretic medication. Most importantly, my patient was breathing better, his vital signs were stable again, and he was not bleeding.

I ventured back to pediatrics to find both my asthmatic girl and her nurse doing fine. I decided to cut back on the Susphrine to see what would happen. I asked the nurse to update me every half hour and as necessary. I needed to take a nap.

As I was making my way down the stairs to do so, my pager went off. The operator reported that somebody wanted me in the emergency room. Off I went to the emergency room on the first floor of the hospital.

I introduced myself to the ER physician, Doctor Francis Apel. I told him I had been paged to the ER. He directed me behind one of the curtains that separated the examination areas.

Behind the curtain was a physician in surgical attire tending to a ten-year-old boy who had been in a car accident. The physician introduced himself as the neurosurgeon on duty for the night. He knew it was late but asked me if I wanted to have some fun.

I informed him that I was on call.

He said, "I know, for pediatrics *and* surgery. This is a *kid* with a *surgical* problem. Do you want to help me?"

I told him that the night had been most eventful for me and that I still had patients that I was monitoring.

He asked me to come to surgery. He told me if all went to hell on the floors, then I could leave at any time. The neurosurgeon explained that he didn't get to have much interaction with interns, and he would like to have more teaching time. He asked me to evaluate his patient and make a diagnosis.

After evaluating the youngster, it was obvious that he had a depressed skull fracture on the right side of his head. The boy was also somnolent suggesting a severe concussion, a brain contusion, or worse. I found no other life-threatening injuries.

The surgeon agreed with my findings. Soon we were off to surgery.

The neurosurgeon and I spent the next few hours lifting the depressed piece of bone off the boy's brain. He even let me remove the bone fragment and the blood clot.

All the while I was in surgery, I had the nurses send in updates on my asthmatic child and my surgical ICU patient. The neurosurgeon noted that I was an obsessive son-of-a-gun.

After the surgery, the neurosurgeon asked me to help with the boy's post-op care.

I agreed. (What else did I have to do?)

Over the subsequent hours, I handled about twenty more intern pages. Fortunately, none required the intense effort of those in the first few hours.

Before I knew it, morning came and my first call night was done. I had not been to bed. About 5 a.m., I checked in on all my patients.

The psychotic man on the twelfth floor slept through the night. I ordered that he only be allowed to eat finger foods; no utensils were allowed!

The morning laboratory data on my surgical patient remained stable. His vital signs were stable. His chest tube was functioning well. His surgeon and I saw him together in the ICU. The surgeon had been doing emergency procedures all night also.

The boy with the skull fracture was sleepy with normal vital signs. He would leave the hospital in a week or so apparently normal.

I decreased or eliminated the medications for my girl with asthma who was breathing famously and wanting some breakfast.

At 6 a.m., my first night of call was over. I showered, had some breakfast, and reviewed pediatric charts for rounds at 7 a.m.

I talked to the three other interns who had been on call. Two told me they slept all night after 10 p.m. The other said he had no calls!

I figured I was the lucky one. I definitely had the opportunity to learn a lot that night!

# Zachariah

At 4:30 a.m. the pediatrics ward was usually quiet except for interns like me. While wandering the halls of pediatrics this particular morning, I heard an annoyingly loud buzzing sound coming from behind the door of the children's play area at the end of the hospital wing. As I walked by the nurses' workstation, I asked the nurse on duty if she heard the obnoxious noise.

She told me that Zachariah was back.

"Who is Zachariah?" I asked

The nurse informed me that Zachariah was just a little boy who had been in the hospital a lot. Apparently, he was a bit of a night owl. He liked to watch TV at night. As long as the nurse could hear the TV, she knew where he was. Zachariah had been up since midnight watching the television.

I thought to myself, "What on earth is the child watching that makes so much noise?" I wandered down the hall to see Zachariah.

Sitting cross-legged in front of the television set was a boy I guessed to be about ten years old. He had the characteristic body and facial features of a child with Down's syndrome. Zachariah was calmly sitting close to the television with the sound turned up to the point that I put my fingers in my ears to dampen the noise. Playing on the television at 4 a.m. was the local television station's test pattern! (This was before all-night cable television.)

I introduced myself to Zachariah as Doctor Ashcraft.

He said, "That's nice."

I asked, "What are you watching on the television?"

Zachariah replied, "Pretty things."

"How long have you been watching the pretty things?" I inquired.

He responded, "Don't know."

I was intrigued with this young fellow in his own little world. I asked him if I could watch television with him.

He said, "Sure, over there." He pointed to a sofa a few feet away and then resumed his intense concentration on the TV test pattern.

Just before 5 a.m., the morning television programming started by removing the test pattern. There was a blank screen for a few moments followed by the playing of "The Star Spangled Banner" while showing a movie of a waving American flag. When the flag movie started, Zachariah stood up, placed his hand over his heart, and smiled while staring at the television set.

When the song was over, Zachariah simply said, "All done!" He then walked to his bed and went to sleep.

I was impressed!

I asked the night nurse to tell me about Zachariah. She told me that he watched the flag at the end of the day, watched the test pattern all night, and went to bed in the morning after the flag waved again. Besides having Down's syndrome with its associated mental retardation, the nurse had no clue about Zachariah's behavior or why he came so often to the hospital.

I never learned about his mysterious illness. However, I always knew when Zachariah was in the hospital.

# Color My World

One thing that children *do not like* is the white attire worn by medical personnel. I observed and appreciated this phenomenon when I was a medical student taking a pediatrics rotation at the Emmanuel Hospital in Portland, Oregon. I asked the head pediatric nurse at Emmanuel why nurses had to wear white uniforms. The answer I received was, "Because."

After several weeks on the pediatrics ward at the Sacred Heart Hospital in Spokane, I made the same observations. I do not know why, but every time I approached an infant in my white intern's jacket, it seemed to me that the infant became more irritable. Whenever a nurse wearing a white uniform cared for a child, the young patient became agitated. If a lab technician arrived in a long white coat, the older pediatric patient would put up quite a fight. Some call this phenomenon the white coat syndrome.

I talked with the pediatric nurses who said they had wanted to change their uniforms for some time. The nurses also told me that the hospital administrator would never allow it. I was reminded that wearing white uniforms in the hospital was a law of nursing that started with Florence Nightingale.

I inquired if any nurse had ever asked the administrator for permission to change their uniforms. The response was always something like, "Are you kidding me?" or "Who would dare?"

I talked with our intern medical director who informed me that the administrator was one tough woman. He suggested that I could talk to her at my own peril. He would remain a neutral observer.

After about four weeks on the pediatrics ward, I garnered the nerve to talk with the hospital administrator. I made an appointment to see her on a Thursday by myself. (I did not want to have anyone else get into trouble if I messed up.) I wrote and rehearsed a speech of reason. I had no idea why I became so nervous, but I did. It was just an issue about clothes. I figured that nobody was going to live or die because a doctor or a nurse wore white clothes. However, I felt it was my issue. It was a nursing issue and a patient care issue.

When I walked into the administrator's office, I was struck by how large and how dark the room was. The administrator was waiting for me at her desk that was illuminated by a single reading light. She asked me to sit in a chair in front of her desk. She said to me, "Doctor Ashcraft, I understand you have an important issue for me."

I did not know how important my issue was compared to running a twelve-story hospital, but I felt I had a positive suggestion regarding the care of the children in her hospital. I presented my prepared remarks. I then thanked the administrator for her time.

She thanked me for my enthusiasm and candor. The administrator told me that she and her staff would take the subject under advisement. She bid me farewell.

I had no idea what to expect for my efforts. However, I had put the topic out for discussion.

When I arrived on the pediatrics floor the next Monday, the nurses were buzzing with excitement as they rummaged through a collection of magazines. When I asked a nurse about the excitement, she pointed to a notice from the hospital administration that morning that was posted on the bulletin board. It stated something like, "Effective immediately, colored attire may be worn by the nursing staff when caring for pediatric patients at Sacred Heart Hospital."

I had no idea if my visit to the administrator prompted the change, but it didn't matter – color was in! The nurses were elated about choosing, buying, and wearing new colored uniforms.

The interns, however, were stuck with their traditional white coats and ties or surgical scrub suits. I figured the system could be pushed only so far at a time.

For my part, I wore colorful bow ties.

# A Sore Throat

John Phillips, M.D., my internal medicine preceptor, who happened to be a hematology specialist, asked me to evaluate a patient for him. He told me that one of his partners had admitted a twenty-six-year-old man from the emergency room early in the morning. Since he was the physician on call for his group this day, Doctor Phillips and I assumed responsibility for the care of this patient. I was told only that the man had a constant sore throat.

I made my way to the internal medicine wing of the hospital where I reviewed the patient's chart from the emergency room. The chart had little useable information except that the man complained of having a severe sore throat for almost two months and that his blood count showed a profound anemia. I garnered from the emergency physician's notes that he admitted the patient just to be sure he did not miss anything serious.

I awakened the young man as I came into the hospital room. I noticed that he appeared profoundly pale and weak (thus validating his anemia). My new patient told me that he had seen three or four different physicians over the previous two months for a severe sore throat. Each time he was briefly examined by the doctor and given a shot of penicillin for a strep throat.

I asked if any of the doctors had done any lab tests or throat cultures.

The man quickly replied, "No."

I asked if he ever felt better after the penicillin shots.

Again he said, "No."

I went through a comprehensive review of the man's medical history including drug use, illnesses, operations, injuries, and a prolonged review of his body systems. The entire history was negative except for the past two months when he had a severe sore throat and fatigue. The man had been a star athlete in high school and college. He told me he always had been healthy as a horse.

My examination revealed no inflammation of the man's throat. However, he had massively enlarged lymph nodes at the angles of his jaws, the back of his neck, in his armpits, and in his groin. I found his spleen to be tender and enlarged during my abdominal examination.

I told the young man that he was weak because he did not have enough blood in his system. I added that I was going to give him some blood that day that should make him feel better. Additionally, I informed him that our team was going to try to determine the cause of his anemia since he gave me no history of blood loss. I also informed him that I would return after Doctor Phillips and our medical team had discussed his case. Finally, I ordered a topical anesthetic medication for his sore throat.

I telephoned Doctor Phillips to inform him of my visit with our new patient. He asked me to come to the hospital's laboratory. He said that he had something very interesting for me to see.

Doctor Phillips was looking into a teaching microscope (one with two sets of optics) when I arrived. After I relayed my history and examination findings to him, Doctor Phillips commended my efforts. He then had me look into the microscope at our patient's blood slide and asked me what I saw. After looking a short time, I described the slide just as I had learned to do in medical school. There were almost no red cells. There were almost no lymphocyte white cells.[13] Only a few platelets existed, and they seemed abnormally large. A normal number of neutrophil white cells were present.

Doctor Phillips noted my description was correct. Then he wanted to know my diagnosis.

I told Doctor Phillips that I did not have a diagnosis, but it was obvious to me that our patient's bone marrow was underperforming for some reason.

He agreed. Doctor Phillips wanted to know what I thought after I added in the fact that enlarged lymph nodes were found on my examination.

I told him that I would consider a lymphoma (a cancer of lymph tissues).

He said, " You're right. What kind?"

I told him I had no idea.

Doctor Phillips said he too didn't know. He told me we needed to perform a bone marrow biopsy and asked if I ever done one.

I told him that I had performed a bone marrow biopsy once on an infant when I was on my pediatrics rotation.

---

[13] Blood contains three basic types of cells. Red blood cells or RBCs carry oxygen. Platelets help blood to clot. There are two types of white cells or WBCs which aid in fighting infections: lymphocytes produce antibodies, and neutrophils consume debris.

Doctor Phillips said he would arrange for his resident hematology fellow[14] to help me with the procedure. In the meantime, I was encouraged to read up on blood cancers for a discussion the next day.

Early the next afternoon, the hematology fellow paged me to our patient's room to perform the biopsy. I had previously talked with the young man and had obtained permission for the procedure.

The hematology fellow seemed a bit put out having to work with an intern.

The bone marrow biopsy procedure involved inserting (more like ramming) a large, heavy gauge hollow needle into the pelvic bone from the backside. A large syringe is then attached to the needle. A significant amount of suction is needed to pull out chunks of bone marrow.

On my first attempt, I was able to aspirate only a few drops of usable material. My second attempt was no better. When my third aspiration yielded only a token more bone marrow, the fellow said to me, "Move aside, intern. Let me show you how it's done."

After three more attempts, he got *nothing*.

I thought to myself, "Hooray!"

He exclaimed, "Well I'll be damned!" He then said, "We're done here. Let's go to the lab."

The technicians in the lab informed us that the slides would not be ready for 24 hours. Therefore, I headed to the library to study.

The next day my patient felt a lot better after receiving eight units of blood. (The human body has 12 to 16 units of blood normally.)

That afternoon I met with Doctor Phillips in the lab. He said, "The nurse told me you had quite a time with my fellow. He does have an attitude, doesn't he? He didn't like being upstaged by an intern. *It was good for him!*"

Doctor Philips had two things for me to see. First was a positive test for infectious mononucleosis (this explained the sore throat). Second was a special type of lymphocyte called a Reed-Sternberg cell that he found after searching a considerable time

---

[14] A fellow is a physician doing graduate training in a subspecialty of medicine. In this case, the fellow was learning hematology, the subspecialty of blood disorders.

through slides of our patient's sparsely populated blood. This cell is diagnostic for Hodgkin's disease (now called Hodgkin's lymphoma). Doctor Phillips told me that our patient appeared to be in an aplastic crisis (when the bone marrow shuts down totally). This was not a good prognostic sign.

Doctor Phillips asked me to consult with a general surgeon about performing a staging laparotomy[15] on our young man soon. Doctor Phillips asked me if I had time to join him when he talked to our patient.

Of course I had time.

Doctor Phillips had spent his entire career talking with patients about cancer issues. Watching him give our young patient really bad news with compassion and understanding impressed me. I thought he was a real pro. I never forgot his bedside manner.

A couple days later my patient had his staging surgery. This revealed an extensive spread of the lymphoma tumor throughout his body. Doctor Phillips labeled his disease as Stage IV Hodgkin's disease with an aplastic crisis. The diagnosis carried a very bad prognosis.

Doctor Phillips transmitted the bad news to our patient and the family members who had come to support him. After considerable discussion, the group decided upon a course of treatment knowing that the outlook was bleak at best. (Today, the five-year cure rate for stage IV Hodgkin's lymphoma is about eighty-five percent.)

On his fifth hospital day, our young patient informed me his sore throat was gone and thanked me. Sadly, on his twentieth hospital day, our patient died from complications associated with his chemotherapy.

I always wondered if this fellow would have fared better if the original physicians had taken more time evaluating his history and his symptoms before administering antibiotics.

This was a good lesson for me: *Listen to the patient!*

---

[15] A staging laparotomy is an exploratory abdominal operation to determine the extent to which a tumor has spread. Today, tumor staging is often done by noninvasive tests such as ultrasound, CT scans, PET scans, etc. However, these tools were not yet in mainstream use when I trained. This surgery is still commonly used today.

# Sightless

I had the opportunity to spend five afternoons during one week of my internship with an ophthalmologist named Harold Jensen. Doctor Jensen informed me that his job was to teach me the basics of opthalmology so I could perform an adequate eye examination on my patients. Doctor Jensen's office was in downtown Spokane. I relished the idea that I could spend some time outside the hospital during the day without being on call.

The first afternoon, Doctor Jensen discussed all his expensive optical equipment with me and then allowed me the opportunity to practice with them as I tried to examine his patients' eyes. I learned about the drugs he used on a regular basis and the drugs with which a primary care physician should become familiar.

The second afternoon, the optician[16] taught me the basics of fitting glasses, taking eye pressures, and performing basic visual field evaluations. After I spent some time attempting to fit an elderly woman with corrective lenses, I had a better appreciation for the expertise required of the optician.

When I came to the office on the third day, Doctor Jensen told me in a nonchalant manner, "Doctor Ashcraft, I have something that you may be interested in seeing." The doctor's eyes pointed toward a man sitting in an examination chair. As we went into the examination room, Doctor Jensen told me this fellow had stopped his motorcycle at the red light outside and right below his office. Doctor Jensen pointed to the intersection right outside his office window. Doctor Jensen said the man noticed that all of a sudden his vision was blurred. He was concerned about being able to drive his motorcycle, and since the office was right there, he just walked in. The patient had arrived no more than ten minutes before me. I was asked to take a look into the man's eyes and report what I saw. Doctor Jensen asked me to start with the man's right eye.

---

[16] An *optician* specializes in the filling of optical prescriptions and products. An *optometrist* diagnoses and treats certain eye conditions, but mostly relating to vision correction. An *ophthalmologist* is a physician specializing in the medical and surgical treatment of eye disorders.

I asked the man if he had any pain.

He said, "No."

I asked the patient if he ever had any eye problems.

Again, he said, "No."

I sensed that I did not have a talkative patient, so I asked him if he had anything medically wrong with him that I should know about.

He said that he had diabetes and took insulin shots.

When I heard this, I thought I knew the answer *before* I examined the man's eyes.

When I looked into the man's right eye, Doctor Jensen asked me what I saw.

I described the anatomy of the eye from front to back just as I was taught the previous two days. I thought the eye appeared absolutely normal and told my preceptor.

He replied, "Absolutely correct! Now, what about the left eye?"

When I started the examination sequence on the left eye, the patient said, "I see nothing."

The patient had no vision in any visual field that I could determine. When I peered into his eye with an ophthalmoscope (a fancy name for a flashlight), I saw nothing. The retina, the back of the eyeball, was totally white. There were no blood vessels to be seen. I told Doctor Jensen that I saw nothing.

He asked me what I thought had happened to the man's eye.

I responded with, "I do not have a clue. I know the eye has no blood supply."

Doctor Jensen retorted, "Absolutely correct. He has no blood supply to his eyeball. He has sustained an acute retinal artery occlusion (blocked artery with a blood clot) with instant blindness. He feels no pain because there are no pain fibers in that part of the eye."

I asked what could be done.

The answer was nothing could be done. The retina died within moments of the artery occlusion. Now our job was to try to find the cause. Doctor Jensen went on to explain to the patient and to me that a cause is often not found. However, we should at least look for one. Doctor Jensen asked the patient if he had anything to do for the afternoon.

The man told us he was in our hands. He was not going to ride his motorcycle to his home in Seattle.

Doctor Jensen took me aside in another room and explained to me that his usual practice would be to send this man to the specialty clinic for further evaluation. However, since I was in the office already and since I was training and accustomed to doing medical evaluations, I might be able to teach him something. Doctor Jensen asked me if I would like to evaluate this man for him.

I agreed.

I escorted the man into another room that was out of the traffic pattern of the office. By taking a detailed history, I learned that the man had been traveling by motorcycle for about a month. He had insulin dependent diabetes; he had been changing the needle and syringe for his insulin about once a week instead of daily. He denied ever injecting illegal drugs, such as heroin or cocaine. He smoked two packages of cigarettes daily. The man thought he was in good shape except for his diabetes.

My examination revealed:

1.  Poor dental hygiene with several large dental cavities plus infected gums.
2. A  heart murmur that the man said he was born with and that had never bothered him.
3.  Small hemorrhages with painless red bumps on the palms of his hands and the soles of his feet.

After putting all the pieces together, I thought the man might have bacterial endocarditis (an infection inside the heart involving the valves) caused by dirty needles and/or infection from his dental disease. The small hemorrhages were classic findings for endocarditis. I knew that a person with a known heart murmur had a greater chance of this malady. Additionally, diabetics seemed to have an increased incidence of the disorder. Unlike this man, patients with endocarditis usually present with a fever, malaise, and a vague illness for several weeks. The small clots that come loose from the heart valve infections usually cause small hemorrhages or strokes. I had not heard of a blood clot to the retinal artery.

Interestingly, I had just completed my rotation in cardiology the previous Friday, and I knew the treatment included multiple weeks of intravenous antibiotics in the hospital after the offending bacteria had been isolated.

After spending several hours with the patient, I presented my hypothesis to Doctor Jensen. I had him listen to the man's heart murmur. I presented the patient's dental infection. Finally, I showed Doctor Jensen the small hemorrhages on the man's palms that are known as Janeway lesions.

He seemed satisfied. He made a call to a cardiologist who had been my preceptor the previous month. The cardiologist arranged for our patient to be evaluated further in the hospital.

On Friday, Doctor Jensen's staff had a small goodbye party at the end of the clinic hours. The doctor told me he had consulted with the cardiologist and the infectious disease expert at the hospital that morning. He told us the specialists called his patient, "A fascinoma, a case of bacterial endocarditis presenting as a retinal artery occlusion."

Doctor Jensen told me that the specialists wanted to write a journal article about our interesting patient.

After clinic, I was off to the hospital. I was on night call in an hour.

I do not know if the patient's case ever reached the medical literature.

# A Mistake

I was at the nurses' station completing my morning paper-work when a female student nurse ran past me crying, "I killed my patient! I killed my patient!"

I had noticed the room from which the student had exited, so I promptly went to the patient's room to see if I could be of assistance. Upon entering the room, I found a middle-aged female patient eating breakfast and watching television. She definitely was alive. She definitely appeared to be in no distress. After I introduced myself, I asked the woman how she felt.

Her response was, "I feel fine. Is that young nurse okay? She was really upset about something."

I reassured the woman that I would find out for her.

I left the patient's room in search of the distraught nursing student. I could hear the young woman's loud wailing coming from a room down the hall. I found her sobbing uncontrollably in a room used by the nurses to prepare medications. When I asked her about the problem, she would only repeat, "I killed my patient!"

I consoled the student and reassured her that I had just seen her patient, and the woman was definitely not dead. She was eating and watching television.

The student nurse cried out, "But she's going to die – and I'm responsible!"

I pleaded with the student for probably five minutes to tell me what she had done. Finally, she said, "I gave her an overdose of medication."

I asked her, "What medication?"

She showed me an ampule of heparin, an anticoagulant[17] medication. She said, "I gave her 100 times the ordered dose in her IV! She is going to bleed to death! It's all my fault!"

Quickly I looked at the doctor's order. It read "Heparin 1000 units/ml (units per milliliter). Put 1.5 ml into IV bottle daily."

This was a common physician order at the time in an attempt to prevent clots in intravenous lines and in patients' arms. Our

---

[17] Anticoagulants are chemicals that inhibit or prevent blood from clotting. Common uses include the treatment of heart rhythm disorders or blood clots. They are used in certain types of surgery to prevent clotting.

hospital was having an upsurge in the number of blood clots in intravenous lines at the time.

The doctor's handwriting on the order form was not very legible. (What a surprise!) I went over the order with the student nurse and asked her about the supposedly fatal error.

She showed me the heparin bottle that she had used and sobbed, "This is 10,000 units per milliliter, not 1,000 units per milliliter. I was supposed to give 1.5 milliliters, but I thought it said 15 milliliters. I gave her 15 milliliters. That's 100 times too much! She is going to bleed to death, and it's all my fault!"

I looked again at the writing on the physician order form and could understand why the student made a mistake. I asked the woman if she had ever heard of protamine sulfate (protamine).

Her reply was, "What?"

Again I asked her if she had you ever heard of the drug named protamine.

She had not.

I then informed her that protamine was the antidote for heparin. Protamine reverses the effects of heparin almost instantly.

She stopped crying as if in disbelief. She asked me, "Are you sure?"

I told her that I was positive.

At that moment, I started to look in the drug cabinet for a bottle of protamine; I did not find one. I called the pharmacy and asked the technician to please send up a bottle of protamine with the package insert to the medical floor promptly. Within a couple minutes a bottle of the drug arrived as requested. I gave the bottle and the literature to the student nurse.

She promptly read about the effects of protamine on heparin. Then the young student nurse withdrew the appropriate amount from the bottle into a syringe. She and I walked down the corridor together to the patient's room to administer the antidote.

The patient smiled as we entered her room and asked the student nurse if she was okay.

The student nurse said that she was fine. The young nurse told the patient that she had given too much medicine earlier. Now she had to give some medicine to reverse it.

The woman, who was not concerned, said, "Do what you have to my dear. Doctor said I'm not going anywhere for a week."

After I watched the student insert the protamine into the intravenous line, I left the room to complete my paperwork.

Soon thereafter, the student, accompanied by her professor, approached me at the nurses' station. She smiled and said, "You saved me. How can I ever repay you?"

I told her that I just happened to know more about heparin than she did that day.

The professor stepped in and stated, "Thank-you. You made this a valuable learning experience. We would like to repay you."

I suggested that cookies always worked for me.

The next morning the two women gave me a plate piled high with cookies. I took a few cookies for myself and left the rest for the regular nursing staff. I attached a note that read, "From the students. Thanks!"

# Seizure

Sometime in mid-afternoon, a young nurse came running out of an obstetric patient's room screaming, "She's having a seizure! Get the popsicle sticks!" She grabbed me as I was walking down the hall and pulled me into the room.

The obstetric personnel were a bit on edge since a pregnant woman experienced not one, but two, seizures the previous week that were associated with a disorder of pregnancy called pre-eclampsia.[18] That particular episode was resolved with an emergency cesarean section on the pregnant mother to deliver the baby. Since then, the OB nurses were ever watchful for any signs that may suggest a seizure in their patients *before* they delivered.

As I came into the patient's room, I saw three young nurses surrounding a young pregnant woman lying in bed. One of the nurses shouted out to me that they were trying to restrain the woman to keep her from hurting herself.

Another added, "It's obvious she's having a seizure! Just look at her!"

I saw a young woman who was no longer pregnant. Her legs were stiff with her toes curled downward. Her arms were rotated inward with her fists clenched. Her jaws were clamped down. Her respiratory status was good. However, the woman was watching me! I knew she couldn't be having a seizure and be alert like this.

I asked the nurses for some history on this patient. I was told that she had delivered her first baby about twelve hours before. There were no problems with the birth. The baby was fine. Another nurse told me that the baby had just been taken back to the nursery after mom's first attempt at breastfeeding. When the young nurse came to take the woman's vital signs, the new mom was having the spell that we were watching.

I knew this was not a seizure. I had seen this condition before when I was taking my psychiatry rotation in medical school. On

---

[18] Pre-eclampsia is a disorder of pregnancy associated with elevated blood pressure, generalized swelling, kidney disease, and nervous system irritability. If the process continues to the point of having seizures, it is termed eclampsia. Both conditions can be fatal. The treatment is the delivery of the baby.

that occasion, the patient was experiencing an acute anxiety attack with hyperventilation (breathing too fast). The hyperventilation changes the acid-base balance in the blood and results in muscle cramping. Since some muscles are stronger than others, the stronger muscles always win. This situation produces the abnormal posturing that the amassed group of medical personnel at the bedside was witnessing with this patient.

The treatment of this disorder is to slow down the breathing by making the patient breathe into a bag or hold their breath. Since this person was unable to hold a bag or her breath, I cupped my hands and placed them firmly over her mouth and nose. Since she was alert, I looked directly into the woman's eyes and explained to her what I was doing.

One of the nurses exclaimed, "Doctor, are you trying to kill her?"

Another nurse ran into the room and shouted, "I have the popsicle sticks!"

Within a minute or so, the woman's arms relaxed. After another few minutes, our patient could move her legs again. All the time, I continued to talk with this young woman to help her relax. After about five minutes, I had this new mom place her own hands over her mouth and asked her to stay that way for another ten minutes by the clock on the wall. I asked one of the nurses to stay with her patient and time her.

Speaking softly through her cupped hands, the new mom told the gathering of people around her bed that she got really flustered trying to breast feed her baby and had feelings that she was already a bad mother.

Upon hearing this, one of the experienced nurses leaned over to the new mom and said, "I've been there. I will help you."

I left the room to notify the woman's obstetrician of this event. Since he was performing an operation, I left a message with the surgery supervisor. I then continued with making rounds on my patients.

The woman's doctor, who was not one of my preceptors, called later and simply said, "Thanks."

# Communication

A Code Blue (medical emergency) sounded about 10 a.m. I had finished rounds on the pulmonary medicine service with my preceptor, Whitney Alan, M.D., and was doing follow-up work for his patients in the medical intensive care unit (MICU). Part of the duties of the intern was to respond to all Code Blue events as a component of the learning process. Therefore, since the alert was nearby and since I personally was not engaged in an emergency, I ran to the patient's hospital room. I arrived at the scene behind another intern. An assortment of nurses, technicians, and more interns followed.

The patient was a middle-aged woman who was unresponsive and had profound respiratory distress. Her face was bluish and covered with hives, and her eyes were nearly swollen shut. As the patient's bed coverings were removed, all could see that she had expanding hives all over her body along with profound body edema (swelling). An attempt by the intern to open the woman's mouth revealed a swollen tongue with a copious amount of saliva pouring out of her mouth. Using my stethoscope, I could hear no air movement in her lungs.

This patient was having an acute allergic reaction called anaphylaxis[19] with throat swelling and airway spasms. I knew that without prompt intervention, this person's throat and lungs would totally obstruct so that she could not breathe, and she would die quickly.

The interns and nurses went into action quickly. The resuscitation protocols had become ingrained into our minds to the point that the process was almost automatic. Someone called for the Crash Cart. (A mobile cart with equipment and medications for an emergency. One such cart was located on each hospital floor and in each ICU.) In rapid succession a tube was placed in the patient's throat to stabilize her airway and artificial ventilation was started; two intravenous lines were inserted for fluids and

---

[19] Anaphylaxis is an immediate hypersensitivity allergic reaction that results in hives, severe tissue swelling, or angioedema, and itching followed by circulatory collapse and shock. It is often accompanied by life-threatening respiratory distress.

medications; oxygen was given through the endotracheal tube; vital signs were taken; a cardiac monitor was attached. The patient was given some adrenalin through both her endotracheal tube and an IV. After all these maneuvers were completed, the patient improved marginally. Another person who was designated as the event recorder documented all of this activity.

One of the interns asked if anyone knew something about the patient, or if anyone knew what happened.

A nurse spoke up and said, "She collapsed soon after I gave her pain pills."

The intern inquired about allergies the patient may have.

The nurse told us that the patient had an allergy to aspirin, and she had a medical bracelet.

The doctor looked at the woman's bracelet and read aloud, "Severe allergy to aspirin. anaphylaxis." He asked the nurse what pills had the patient received.

The nurse responded with, "Doctor, I gave her two Empirin #3 tablets."

He exclaimed, "Oh, Christ, that's aspirin with codeine! Let's get her to the ICU now!"

The nurse looked tearful and shocked. She whimpered, "I just gave what the doctor ordered!"

The woman was transferred in critical condition to the MICU where she was placed on a mechanical ventilator. Two MICU nurses and I remained to care for this patient after everyone else left. Soon, Doctor Alan appeared. He said somebody had called his office and told him to come to the ICU now. He cancelled his office patients for the morning and ran to the hospital.

Doctor Alan and I evaluated the patient, determined that she continued to have severe airway spasm, and discussed our therapeutic options. As we were talking, the ventilator alarms sounded showing too much pressure. This usually meant either a mucus plug in a large airway or, more commonly, a collapsed lung caused by the ventilator. A prompt evaluation with a stethoscope revealed no air movement on the left side of the chest. We knew it would take at least fifteen minutes to get a chest x-ray completed. Doctor Alan asked me to put a needle into the left side of her chest anteriorly medially in the third intercostal space (medical speak for in the front, in the middle below the collar bone, below the third rib).

I inserted a large hollow needle into the assigned spot. Instantly, we heard a rush of air from the needle confirming a pneumothorax[20] and the ventilator alarms stopped. The needle was only a temporary fix for the problem, however. The hole in the lung would require several days to heal, so I inserted a chest tube near the location of the needle and connected it to a continuous suction to keep the lung inflated.

Over the next several hours, Doctor Alan and I tried multiple medication maneuvers to halt the woman's profound allergic reaction. Finally, after about four hours of intense effort, our patient's airway spasm started to abate. Doctor Alan decided to keep the woman sedated and attached to the ventilator overnight just in case something else unexpected happened.

Since I was on the pulmonary medicine service and since I knew the patient's problems the best, I had the honor of staying with her all night. (It was not my call night.) During the evening, I had an opportunity to review the patient's chart. The doctor's order sheet plainly stated in the doctor's handwriting:

*Allergy:* Aspirin - anaphylaxis and angioedema!

Just below this in a list of orders was:

Empirin #3 tabs i or ii q4-6h pain (aspirin with codeine 1-2 tabs every 4-6 hours for pain).

*This was an obvious mistake.*

The order form went to the pharmacy where the pharmacist supposedly checked the chart for medication allergies and then filled the medication drawer for the patient with Empirin #3 for pain.

*This was another obvious mistake.*

The nurse, who supposedly double-checked the order sheet and the medications, did not know that Empirin #3 contained aspirin. Even though she was aware the patient had a severe allergy to aspirin, the nurse, in her ignorance or haste, gave it to the patient anyway.

*This was a third obvious mistake.*

The patient's doctor came in to see her in the MICU that evening. We talked about her episode. When I showed him what

---

[20] A pneumothorax, or collapsed lung, is a potentially serious condition in which the lung becomes perforated and air leaks into the chest cavity. The collapsed lung cannot re-inflate unless the leaked air is removed.

I had gleaned in the chart, he just said, "Oh, for Christ's sake!" and left the MICU.

Fortunately, the woman's condition improved hourly through the night. During our MICU rounds at 7 a.m., Doctor Alan decided to wean the patient from the ventilator and her sedation because she was stable and showed no signs of airway spasms.

Over the lunch hour, I extracted the woman's airway tube. The first words out of her mouth were, "Where's my lawyer!" After a few moments elapsed, she said, "I want my lawyer here right now!"

Physically, my patient fared well afterward. She spent several more days in the MICU before her chest tube could be removed. I observed several men in expensive suits come to visit with her. I also saw the hospital administrator come with others to visit with all of them at the bedside.

I was asked to testify before a medical staff investigative committee before the patient left the MICU. I do not know the legal result of this episode. However, I do know that there was a serious lack of communication among the parts of this woman's health care team. These included the doctor, the pharmacy, and the nurse. None of these professionals paid attention to the needs of their mutual patient nor did they pay attention to their own colleagues. Their combined mistakes nearly cost this patient her life but produced more valuable lessons for me.

# First Job

"Try not to become a man of success but a man of value."

Albert Einstein

# Snakebite

I had been in Lusk, Wyoming, in the National Health Service Corps as a general medical officer for less than a month. I was just out of training and green as grass. Midday on a Saturday in July I received a call from a nurse at the hospital who informed me that she had a confirmed snakebite coming in. The victim lived a distance from town and would arrive in about ninety minutes.

I told the nurse that I would come to the emergency room right away to make sure everything was there that we might need. (Having been in town just a short time, I had already ascertained that the small hospital lacked many things that I thought I needed.) Additionally, I knew essentially nothing about snakebites except that they were caused by snakes and were rarely fatal.

After I arrived at the hospital, the nurse told me that the victim was Henry Eichwald. His wife Martha had called in the incident. The pair ranched about eighty miles outside of town in the real boondocks. The nurse reconfirmed the estimated arrival time to be about an hour. I figured that I had plenty of time to read about snakebites in my medical texts that I kept in the hospital as our medical library. I learned that rattlesnake bites are usually superficial wounds, not deep; about half of the bites never have venom; the human injury from trying to suck out the poison usually produces more problems than the actual bite; and only about one percent of actual bites with venom are fatal. Antivenom should be given with all confirmed bites, however, since there is no way to tell which bites inject poison into the victim. One textbook had a step-by-step care plan for snakebites.

I went to the nurse and inquired about the location of the snake anti-venom kit. I thought that since the area was full of rattlesnakes, a snakebite kit would be a standard item in the hospital.

The nurse led me to the pharmacy where we started to look for a snakebite kit. We did not find the kit. We looked in the drawers at the nursing station without success. We then went to the emergency room drug cabinet and again had no luck.

The nurse knew the hospital had a kit, but she didn't know where it had been stored.

After a few moments she thought of another place to look. Off we went toward the ambulance garage. We met one of the ambulance drivers there who told us that he last saw the kit in the emergency room in the closet with the things that never get used.

Again the nurse and I ventured into the emergency room. Behind an unmarked cabinet door we found a collection of *unused stuff* including a snakebite kit that was five years outdated.

The nurse quipped, "I guess it isn't used much."

I figured I should have a recent snakebite kit available so I called the hospital in Torrington, Wyoming, which was about fifty miles away, to ask if they had a kit. Indeed they did have an in-date kit, and the nurse on duty said she would send it by courier ASAP. I thanked the nurse for her efforts and hung up the phone.

About now I heard a call over the intercom, "Doctor Ashcraft, the snakebite is here."

I looked at the clock. The arrival of the victim was thirty minutes ahead of schedule. I went promptly to the emergency area, which was not far away, and encountered considerable commotion. Martha was crying and screaming that Henry was going to die. She had been the driver and left the pickup running at the emergency entrance. Henry was yelling at Martha, but she wasn't listening to him. The nurse had gone into a full resuscitation mode without examining the patient. It was a bewildering scene.

I observed that Martha was a large muscular woman who was both taller and heavier than her husband Henry. He was slim and about five feet six inches by my estimation.

After I got everyone calmed down so we could converse, I simply stated, "Can you tell me what happened?" All at once the yelling, screaming, and crying started again.

I asked the nurse to talk to Martha in another room while I examined Henry and heard his side of the story.

Henry told me that indeed he was out in the barnyard doing chores when a rattlesnake struck at him. However, he told me the snake bit through his Levi's and hit his boot. But, he was never bitten! However, Martha came around the corner of the barn, saw the snake holding onto Henry's pants, and apparently freaked out. Henry stated that Martha essentially dragged him into the pickup, and she headed out across the fields very fast. Martha called in the event with their two-way radio as she was driving. Henry said, "I thought I was going to die in that damn truck. She would not slow down. She would not listen to me!"

The nurse came in to tell me that Martha was beside herself and only wanted to know if Henry was going to make it.

Henry chimed in, "Not if I ride with her in that truck again! She could've killed me!"

I asked Henry for permission to examine him, and he agreed. I saw two puncture holes in his pants near his right ankle. I saw two small scratches on his boot below the puncture holes. These findings verified Henry's story of the non-bite. Additionally, I noticed multiple superficial and a few deeper abrasions on his thighs, calves, and one forearm.

When I asked Henry about these injuries he said, "I got those when Martha drug me to the truck!"

Martha could not stay away and came into the examination room to see what was happening. When she saw Henry's legs she exclaimed, "Honey, did I do that. I didn't mean to. I am so sorry." She then started to cry again and gave Henry a big bear hug.

The nurse and I evaluated, cleaned, and bandaged Henry's wounds.

After we reassured Martha that Henry was going to be all right and that he did not get bitten by a snake, she asked, "I guess I can take him home now?"

Henry quickly responded with, "Not on your life woman. You nearly killed me! I'll drive home after I get a drink, or two! And, we'll take the highway this time!"

The pair was sent home with wound care instructions for Henry. I asked them to take their time and to drive carefully back to their ranch.

I called the Torrington hospital about their snakebite kit. Since their kit had not yet been sent, I cancelled my request. Our nurse told me that she would order a new snakebite kit in the morning.

I checked Henry's wounds a week or so later, and they had healed just fine. Henry told me that Martha went out and killed the snake. He said Martha beat the snake until there was nothing left of it.

We both laughed.

# Rash

After playing in an intramural basketball game in the sixth grade, I noticed a spot of irritated skin in front of my left hipbone. Since I was always getting skin bumps and abrasions, the rash seemed to be no real issue. Besides with time, the irritated skin always got better.

This spot of red, irritated skin, however, never went away. Over the next several years, my skin became quite sensitive to harsh clothes so I could not wear Levi jeans like my brothers. Tight fitting clothes left red pressure marks that remained. Since my mother had sensitive skin, my parents paid little attention to my rashes. Besides, we had no money to waste just to see a doctor for a rash.

Doctors observed the rash when I had pre-sports examinations. Most of them called the spots on my skin either eczema or a strawberry rash. As I recall, these doctors usually encouraged me to apply moisturizing creams and to avoid taking hot baths. These treatments were not helpful.

When my younger brother developed severe acne as a teenager, my parents took him to see a dermatologist in Billings. On one of these occasions, when I was a junior in high school, my mother asked me to accompany her when she took my brother to one of his dermatology appointments. While my brother was being examined for his acne, my mother asked the skin doctor if he would mind looking at me *while I was there*. The physician, named Doctor Nils, examined me briefly and asked me to return later that afternoon for a more thorough examination.

Over the next four years or so, Doctor Nils tried to figure out my skin problem, but he did not succeed. Doctor Nils scraped, biopsied, evaluated, and cultured my skin, but he never determined a cause. He prescribed creams, ointments, injections, vitamins, and diets to make a difference, but none of these helped. Doctor Nils gave my skin problem many names but none was a definitive diagnosis.

Unfortunately, the week after he told me that he thought we were finally making some progress with finding out what was wrong with my skin, Doctor Nils died suddenly. I was now a senior in college. My areas of rash were no worse, but they were no better. Additionally, my skin sensitivity was getting worse. After I retrieved my records from Doctor Nils' office a short time later, I made an appointment to visit a new dermatologist at the Billings Clinic who had just completed his training.

My initial visit with Doctor Thomas was scheduled to last fifteen minutes. I left almost two hours later. Doctor Thomas reviewed Doctor Nils' notes. He scraped and pinched my skin until it bled. He examined my skin lesions under different colored lights. He finally told me, "I have no idea what's wrong with you. You're fascinating." Doctor Thomas asked if he could take biopsies of several different skin lesions. He told me he wanted his pathologists to look at them. Also, he wanted to send samples to his dermatology professors to get their opinions.

I agreed, and Doctor Thomas took multiple biopsies of my skin for evaluation under a microscope. He asked me to return in a month to get the results.

When I returned as requested, Doctor Thomas told me, "Nobody knows exactly what you have. The best we could come up with is chronic inflammatory eczema with capillary fragility or chronic pigmented purpura[21] with atrophic changes."

When I asked what the big words meant, he told me that they just described my skin in medical terms. They were not a diagnosis.

When I asked how I should treat the skin lesions, he had no specific recommendations other than what I had been told previously. Doctor Thomas knew that I had been accepted to medical school. When I told him that I would be attending the University of Oregon Medical School in a few months, Doctor Thomas asked me to see Doctor Rockwell, a world-famous dermatologist and the chairman of the dermatology department at the Oregon medical school. Doctor Thomas told me that if his professors came up with anything else he would contact me.

Several weeks into my first quarter as a medical student, I ventured into the dermatology department as a patient. Since I

---

[21] Purpura relates to a small hemorrhage beneath the skin that may be caused by many factors.

was a medical student, I received royal treatment from the office staff. When a group of young doctors came into my cubicle to examine me again, I was scraped, pinched, cultured, examined under lights, and biopsied. I could tell by the looks in their eyes that these doctors didn't have a clue what was wrong with me.

After waiting about half an hour in the cubicle, the entire team reappeared along with their preceptor, Doctor Rockwell. After detailing my history and their examination findings to Doctor Rockwell, he carefully examined my skin lesions. He then said, "Poikiloderma, obvious Poikiloderma,"[22] and walked out without saying another word.

The younger doctors repeated, "Ah, Poikiloderma!" and left the room.

I was impressed. Doctor Rockwell knew my diagnosis by just looking at my skin. Finally, I had a diagnosis. I had no idea what it meant, but my skin problem finally had a name.

Soon thereafter, a dermatology resident named Doctor Story talked to me about my skin disorder. Doctor Story gave the full name of the disorder as *poikiloderma atrophicus vasculare,*[23] a skin problem that usually arises in people over sixty years of age. She also told me that it is not a disease but just another description of the skin. However, it could be a precursor to other skin problems. The resident doctor gave me their plan of treatment, and since I was a medical student, the treatments would not cost me a penny. Afterward, senior medical students took more biopsies, scrapings, and cultures.

During my next four years in medical school, I was treated with steroids, lights of different types for varying durations, and creams of different types. None of the treatments made me better, but my skin did not seem to get any worse either. Upon leaving medical school, a dermatology faculty member told me that my skin problem would never be more than a minor inconvenience.

My skin issue remained stable during my internship until April of 1975. While I was experiencing my dermatology rotation

---

[22] Poikiloderma is a skin condition characterized by pigmentary and atrophic changes that gives the skin a mottled appearance.

[23] Poikiloderma atrophicus vasculare is a chronic skin disorder that may be localized or generalized. The skin becomes friable and cigarette paper thin. It most commonly occurs in the elderly. The disorder may or may not be a precursor of more serious skin disorders.

in late April, my skin became quite irritated. I asked my seventy-year-old dermatologist preceptor, Doctor Buford "B.D." Runyan, to evaluate my skin lesions. After I presented Doctor Runyan my history with dermatologists, he looked at my skin and wanted to know how long my skin had this appearance.

Since my skin had been really irritated for only a few months, I said, "A few months."

He asked, "No, I mean, when did it start?"

I told him the rash started when I was about twelve years old.

Doctor Runyan replied, "Amazing."

I asked him what he thought the rash was.

Instead of answering my question, Doctor Runyan asked if he could obtain a few biopsies to take back with him to the University of Oregon Medical School the next week. He informed me that he was a visiting professor there, and he thought my skin would provide an interesting case study.

I agreed to the biopsies.

He took fourteen skin samples from all over my body.

About four weeks later, just before I graduated from my internship, Doctor Runyan asked me to come to his office. He reported that my skin biopsies showed a microscopic abnormality that was consistent with a cancer called mycosis fungoides. Doctor Runyan also told me that he had seen mycosis fungoides previously but only in old men. The condition was rare; in my age group, the disease was almost unheard of. Doctor Runyan thought that my chances of having mycosis fungoides were at least a million to one.

Now I had a diagnosis.

Since he knew I would be entering the National Health Service Corps in Wyoming, Doctor Runyan told me to contact Doctors Eastman and Gold in the dermatology department at the University of Colorado for an appointment when my wife and I were settled in Wyoming. They were part of a nationwide collaborative study of the disease.

I met with the doctors at the University of Colorado in the summer of 1975. They confirmed my diagnosis. The doctors wanted me to begin a regimen of topical nitrogen mustard chemotherapy. The senior dermatology resident informed me, "If this does not work, your life expectancy is less than three years."

I obtained a month's supply of the nitrogen mustard from the study group and started to apply the stuff to all my skin twice daily. After I developed severe side effects to the medicine, the doctors reduced the dose to once daily.

Within a month, my skin lesions were almost gone. After a few more biopsies were obtained to record the effects of the chemotherapy, I was asked to return every four to six months. The doctors told me that since I was part of a clinical trial, they had no idea when to stop my treatments if I did well. However, after eighteen months of chemotherapy and essentially normal biopsies for over a year, the doctors told me to stop the medication. One of the investigators told me, "Your chance of dying from the medicine is now far greater than dying from your cancer. You'll die from something else." They asked me to come back in five years, or if I got worse again.

I returned in five years to be told, "Your cancer is gone. Come back if you want to see us or if we can be of assistance again."

As the years passed, mycosis fungoides was determined to be a type of non-Hodgkin's lymphoma. It is now called cutaneous T-cell lymphoma. The diagnosis remains difficult to confirm and is quite rare. This type of cancer occurs usually in the elderly as the body's immune system weakens. About 800 to 1,000 cases occur per year in the United States with an incidence of about four cases per million people worldwide. For children, like me when I displayed the first skin signs, the incidence of the disease is about 0.2 cases per million, or only sixty childhood cases per year in the United States.

My original rash occurred over fifty years ago, so I guess I too am a fortunate cancer survivor.

# Hubby Hives

Jeanette was a young woman in her early twenties who came to the emergency room late one autumn evening complaining that she was allergic to her husband. She told me that she and her husband had been married for only a few months. Each time they were intimate, Jeanette developed a rash and severe itching "down there." She denied having had premarital sexual relations with her husband who was about five years older, but they had come close.

I asked what she meant by come close.

Jeanette explained that before getting married her husband had ejaculated during lovemaking, but "on the outside of me only!" She pronounced firmly, "He was never inside of me if that's what you mean!" Jeanette denied developing a rash anywhere during these episodes.

I asked Jeanette if she had allergies.

She related that she did not know of any.

I asked Jeanette if she and her husband were using any kind of contraception such as diaphragms, condoms, foams, etc.

Jeanette replied emphatically, "Nothing goes inside of me except my husband!"

My examination of Jeanette revealed redness and hives on her pubic area, on her inner thighs, and inside her vagina. I found a similar rash on the palms of her hands. I thought this was a classic clinical presentation for a contact dermatitis rash.

While she was in the emergency room, I had Jeanette wash the involved skin areas with soapy water and then apply cool compresses. Her itching improved dramatically.

I obtained some blood for testing and then gave Jeanette a prescription for an antihistamine that she was to take daily for a few days. Additionally, I gave her some samples of a cortisone cream that I asked her to apply to the irritated areas three times a day for a week. I knew Jeanette was a newlywed, but I still asked her to refrain from having sex with her husband until I saw her in a week.

She agreed.

Most of the rash had resolved when Jeanette returned to the clinic a week later,

I asked Jeanette if she and her husband had sex during the interim.

She said, "No." Jeanette then became quite emotional. Holding back tears, she told me that they had taken a shower together, and the rash came back on her hands. Now Jeanette was convinced that she was allergic to her husband. She was beside herself.

I knew that something in this scenario just did not fit, but I did not know what. I knew that Jeanette developed a rash for some reason. I was not convinced that she was allergic to her husband.

One of the first things my wife Kay and I learned when we arrived in Lusk, Wyoming, was that the small town was home to a famous madam and her house of prostitution. We also learned that the town's citizens had tried before to eliminate the madam's enterprise. Since the madam owned the water rights to the town, she just turned off the town's water spigot in retaliation to their protests. The uproar vanished when the town had no water.

I called the husband a few days after Jeanette's latest visit to get his side of his wife's dilemma. After some intensive questioning, the husband confessed to having a long-term relationship with one of the girls. He also admitted to using condoms faithfully to prevent getting a disease. The husband admitted visiting his friend several times a week for several years before he got married. He continued this relationship after his marriage. He told me his wife did not know of his infidelity.

I told the husband that I had become convinced that his wife was extremely sensitive to the latex in his condoms. An allergy to latex was the only thing that made any sense to me. I advised him that his continued use of condoms would only prolong his wife's misery. Additionally, his wife would surely find out about his secret soon. I told the husband that I would discuss my suspicions with his wife if she developed a rash again.

The husband nodded that he understood what I was saying.

I had the opportunity to see Jeanette several more times over the next few months. She reported that her rash had gone away completely and that she must not be allergic to her husband after all.

# A Dilemma

Doctor Berryman and I had been in Lusk, Wyoming, for only several months. The volume of patients we saw in our National Health Service Corps clinic had rapidly increased to almost twice the volume seen by our predecessors. The clinic became profitable for the first time in its history.

About three o'clock one afternoon Margo, my nurse, informed me that my last patient for the day was in examination room 2. This seemed odd to me because our clinic was usually busy until 5 p.m. I must have given Margo a curious stare, because she told me that the patient requested a *very long* visit. She made sure that the two of us had plenty of time to deal with the patient's issues. Since our clinic employees knew just about everyone in the area, I figured that Margo already knew something about my patient that I would soon discover.

As I entered the examination room, I met Janet Adams, a middle-aged woman, for the first time. Janet informed me that she lived near a town about fifty miles away and her work brought her to Lusk about two days per month. Janet said that she was the director of Planned Parenthood for our region of Wyoming.

To learn more about my new patient, I asked Janet what her duties entailed.

She informed me about the objectives of Planned Parenthood and the information they provided for contraception and adoptions. Additionally, she emphasized more than once that Planned Parenthood was against abortions for any reason. Janet informed me that she had worked for Planned Parenthood for almost twenty years and had advanced through the ranks to her current position.

I congratulated Janet on her achievements.

Upon further questioning I learned that Janet and her husband married when she was eighteen. The pair had three children, the youngest was a senior in high school. Janet expressed pride in the accomplishments of her kids and her husband. She and her husband were looking forward to being empty nesters after her youngest daughter graduated from high school in the spring.

Finally, I asked Janet how I could be of assistance.

Abruptly, she started to cry hysterically. She exclaimed, "I'm pregnant! I don't know how, but I'm pregnant! This just can't be! I've had an IUD for years! What am I going to do? I'm over forty years old. I'm too old to have a baby!"

I asked Janet if she was sure about her pregnancy.

She told me that she had done the test in her office three times the day before.

I inquired if she had told her husband about the pregnancy.

Still crying, Janet whimpered that she had not told him.

I asked Janet how she wanted me to help her.

She said, "I don't know. I didn't sleep all night. I know my options, but I don't like any of them." After a pause for a few moments, Janet continued with, "I guess I just need some guidance. I don't want anyone to know about this until they have to."

I told Janet, "Well, you already know you have just two options. Either you have a baby or you don't. If you have a baby, you can keep it or you can give it away. The choice is yours and only yours."

As I talked, Janet became quiet and sobbed. I told Janet that I was going to leave the examination room for a few minutes so she could have some time to compose herself. I then left the room.

When I exited the examination room, Margo was waiting for me in the hallway. She wondered how my patient was doing as if she already knew Janet's problem.

I told Margo that I didn't know yet.

After a few minutes, I reentered the room to find Janet still crying but more composed. I asked her if her IUD had fallen out.

She didn't think so. The IUD was inserted after her youngest child was born, and this child was now a senior in high school.

Then I asked Janet about was the last time she checked for the IUD string?

Janet said, "I haven't felt it for years." After a few moments she added, "I know I should have had it changed every five years, but I just never got around to it."

I asked Janet if she knew what type of IUD she had because a certain type called a Dalkon Shield was associated with many complications.

She did not know.

I told Janet that we should find out if her IUD was still in place. If the IUD was still in her uterus, her pregnancy was already at risk for infection and other complications. I suggested that I be allowed to search for the IUD while she was still in the office.

Janet agreed.

During my examination of Janet's uterus, I could neither see nor locate the IUD string or the device itself. I told Janet that I would have to take an x-ray of her pelvis to find the IUD. I told her that the picture could be taken right away at the hospital.

She agreed.

After the x-ray was completed, I showed Janet that her IUD, which was called a Lippe's Loop, was in her uterus, but it was lying sidewise.

She wanted to know what to do next.

I suggested that Janet discuss her situation with her husband while I consulted several obstetricians about her predicament. I suggested another visit the next day. She nodded in agreement.

The next day Janet came to the office without her husband. Apparently he wanted Janet to have an abortion, but she would not, or could not, consider it. Janet had been preaching against abortions for any reason for more than twenty years and felt she could not go against everything she had taught. She could not go against her religious beliefs. The result was a terrible quarrel between the two.

The physicians I consulted suggested that the IUD be removed early in the pregnancy to prevent almost certain complications. The specialists all noted that the risk for a spontaneous abortion after the removal of the IUD was high. However, they also offered that losing an early pregnancy is better than losing a term infant and possibly a mother. I gave this information to Janet.

Janet told me that she was not ready to make a decision. Besides, she had to consult with her husband. Janet told me that she would let me know her decision. She just didn't know when.

About ten days passed before Janet telephoned the clinic. She asked me to arrange for the removal of the IUD as soon as possible before she changed her mind. Within a few minutes, I arranged for the procedure to be done at our hospital the next morning. (In our small hospital, this was not an easy task because our facility did not have a designated surgical team or an anesthetist.) Janet would be away from her hometown, and, I hoped, her situation would remain confidential.

Janet concurred with my plans.

The next morning Janet came to the hospital escorted by her husband. Janet told me, "Doctor Ashcraft, I can't believe in my heart what I'm doing is right, but for me and my family, it's the right thing to do. It's in God's hands now."

I just listened.

In the operating room, I removed the IUD that was stuck into the wall of the uterus. Additionally, I appreciated no signs of an obvious miscarriage.

Afterward I talked with Janet and her husband about my findings. I told them that I did not know if the pregnancy, which was now about ten week's gestation, would survive. The nurse gave Janet instructions to see either me in about a week.

Several days later Janet called to tell me that she had suffered a miscarriage and that she was feeling fine.

Months passed before Janet returned to the clinic. She said that she just wanted to say thank-you to my staff and me. Janet told me that she had a tough time emotionally after the procedure and the miscarriage. However, she learned that there may be times for an abortion. Janet told me that her Planned Parenthood discussions with pregnant girls now freely entertained abortion as an alternative, the last possible alternative.

# Tuckered

Quite early one weekend morning, Harvey Delayne drove for an hour over country roads to get to the Niobrara County Hospital Emergency Room. The emergency room nurse working the night shift awakened me when she telephoned about Harvey's condition. She told me that a man was in her emergency room complaining of being "plum tuckered." She said the man informed her that he was "just all in."

When I questioned the nurse about the man being more specific about how he felt, the nurse replied, "Doctor Ashcraft, you got it from the horse's mouth. I can't tell you anything more specific."

After the nurse assured me that her patient did not appear to be in acute distress, I told her I would be in the hospital in a few minutes. I asked her to administer some oxygen to our patient.

Upon my arrival at the emergency room I saw my patient sitting on an examination bed with an oxygen mask attached to his face. When I reviewed the nurse's notes on the emergency room form, I noticed that my patient was seventy years old. His vital signs were normal, and his pulse was regular. The nurse had written his main complaint as being plum tuckered out. After introducing myself to Mr. Delayne, I asked what brought him to the hospital.

He replied, "When I got up to do my chores yesterday morning, I was plum tuckered. I moped around my place all day yesterday. I even went to bed early last night. This morning I felt puny again. So, here I am." After a short pause and before I could say another word, Harvey said, "Doc, I feel pretty darn good right now. I think I'm wasting your time. I think I'll just go home and feed my critters." Harvey then took off his oxygen mask, grabbed his coat, and headed toward the emergency room door.

I asked Mr. Delayne if he was sure he didn't want me to examine him first.

He replied, "Nope. I feel good now. I'd just be wasting your time. Thanks anyway, Doc." With that, Harvey Delayne walked to his pickup truck and drove away.

I asked the nurse if she knew him.

All she knew for sure was that Harvey was a widower who ranched about forty miles from town.

Since I was already fully awake by now, I decided to stay at the hospital and make morning rounds on my patients.

Several hours later the dayshift nurse summoned me to the emergency room to see a patient. She told me that two men brought in a third gentleman who had collapsed at a local cafe while eating his breakfast. She told me that she thought he looked okay but thought I should check him over before he went home.

I asked if the man had been drinking.

The nurse said she didn't think so unless it was coffee.

I told the nurse that I would be there soon and started to walk toward the emergency room that was just down the hall in our small hospital.

When I turned the corner into the emergency room I saw Harvey Delayne again. As before he was sitting on the bed with an oxygen mask on his face. I said something like, "Mr. Delayne, you just couldn't get enough of this place could you?"

He replied, "I don't know what happened, Doc. I was almost done with my breakfast and my lights went out. When I woke up, two big fellas were hauling me in here."

Again, Mr. Delayne indicated that he felt fine and had to go home to feed his animals. Harvey stood up and was preparing to leave as before when I put my hand on his shoulder and said, "Mr. Delayne, fool me once shame on you; fool me twice shame on me. You don't get to leave until I check you over."

Harvey gave me a disgusted look and said, "Okay, have it your way." He then lay back on the examination table.

When I asked Harvey about what he meant by plum tuckered out, he told me that he had little energy. He got tired doing his normal chores. He was even tired when he woke up in the morning.

When I asked if he had ever been sick, Harvey replied, "Only when I got the fever as a young boy."

In response to my questions about ever having any injuries or operations, Harvey said, "Did you ever see a rodeo cowboy who didn't get hurt? Hell yes I got hurt, lots of times, but none of them did me in."

When I asked Harvey if he had been sick in any way recently, he wanted to know what I meant by recently.

I asked if he had been ill within the past two months.

Harvey thought a short time and said, "Nope, I don't think so." After a few moments, he added, "Well, I did have a bad bout of indigestion with gas and bloating about a month ago."

I asked him to tell me more about that episode.

Harvey continued to tell me that he had bad gas pains one night after supper. He admitted to being a terrible cook and figured he had consumed some tainted food. The discomfort lasted most of that night but was gone by morning. Harvey said he had been fine since then until the past few days.

When I asked Harvey if he ever had anything wrong with his heart, he answered emphatically, "No!"

While my patient was talking, I was thinking that he might have suffered a heart attack with an atypical presentation several weeks before (the gas and bloating). As a result, he may be having some heart failure with mild exertion (feeling puny, plum tuckered out). Finally, Harvey said he felt better after he received oxygen. I thought my theory made perfect sense if his damaged heart was oxygen deprived and he felt better after receiving some oxygen.

When I examined Harvey with my stethoscope, I heard fine crackling noises in his lungs when he took a deep breath. This finding suggested a fluid accumulation. His heart examination revealed a normal rhythm, but I heard an extra heart sound called an S-4 gallop. A damaged heart under stress often makes this sound. Except for arthritic changes in his joints, I found no other significant problems that would explain Harvey's symptoms.

I told Harvey that I wanted to do a test on him.

He wanted to know what kind of test.

I told him that I wanted him to go for a little walk with me down the hall.

Harvey said, "Hell Doc, I can do that all day. Let's get to it. I've got critters to feed."

With that I removed the oxygen from Harvey's face. I had the nurse obtain a blood oxygen saturation reading before we started. (This was done by attaching a small electronic device onto a finger.) The meter read ninety-eight percent, a normal result.

Harvey stood up and off we went down the hospital hallway.

Harvey had walked only a short distance when he started to feel puny again and asked if he could sit down. Since we were next to the nursing station by now, I had Harvey support himself on the countertop. The nurse noted that his blood oxygen level had dropped to eighty-six percent.

I thought to myself, "Aha! I'm right."

The nurse had a nursing aide bring a wheelchair for Harvey, and we escorted him back to the emergency room where the oxygen mask was reapplied.

I told Harvey that I thought he was having some heart problems and that I wanted to do a couple more tests. I assured him that the testing wouldn't hurt.

Harvey nodded in agreement.

I performed an electrocardiogram (ECG), or heart tracing. The ECG revealed evidence for an inferior wall heart attack (on the bottom and back heart walls) that had occurred some time in the past. I saw no evidence on the ECG for any acute process. However, there was evidence for heart strain.

A chest x-ray revealed evidence for congestive heart failure.

After the tests were completed and I had evaluated them, I advised Harvey that I thought he experienced a heart attack several weeks before and that his heart was showing signs of failing a bit.

Harvey asked, "Okay, Doc, how long have I got?"

I replied, "Once we get you tuned up, you may live another twenty years. However, I think you need to stay in the hospital for a while."

Harvey wanted to know how long he would have to stay in the hospital because he had critters to feed.

I suggested that he should plan on staying in the hospital at least a week to start.

Harvey said, "Fair enough." He then asked for a telephone. When the nurse retrieved the phone, Harvey promptly telephoned a neighbor. He said, "Hey, Bud. This here's Harvey. Say, I'm in the Lusk hospital, and the doc here says I've got some trouble with my ticker. Can you watch my place and feed my critters for a week?"

When the neighbor agreed to feed his animals, Harvey said, "Hey Bud, you're the best. I owe you one."

Afterward, I admitted Harvey to the hospital. After receiving oxygen, diuretics to help remove excess fluid, and, most importantly, quality rest for about a week, Harvey Delayne went home feeling and functioning quite well. I sent Harvey home with a program for heart rehabilitation that he could do at his home that incorporated his farm chores and walking around his land. Bud the neighbor agreed to help Harvey with his farm chores for another month.

About a month later I saw Harvey in the clinic for a follow-up visit. I asked him how he was doing.

Harvey said he never felt better.

After my examination, which was now normal, I asked Harvey if he had suffered any more spells since he went home when he felt puny or plum tuckered out.

Harvey just said, "Nope."

# Off to Work

Whenever you do a thing, act as if all the world were watching.

Thomas Jefferson

# A Toothache

During the spring planting season in 1976, sixty-seven-year-old Otis Yorgason developed a toothache from a bad wisdom tooth. The pain did not bother him all the time, so Otis did not seek treatment from a dentist. The pain persisted off and on through the summer months. Some days Otis complained bitterly to his wife about the pain in his tooth. Despite his wife's insistence to, "Get the darn thing pulled out and taken care of once and for all," Otis always had an excuse not to see the dentist. Besides, the pain was not present all the time. The toothache always subsided after a shot (or two) of whiskey before bedtime. Otis had determined that the pain came and went depending upon what he ate. Sometimes he would have a toothache all day; sometimes he wouldn't have pain for a week or so.

One autumn day after the wheat and corn crops had been harvested, and before the fall fieldwork had started, the toothache returned with a vengeance. Otis complained all day, and his wife demanded that he drive the forty miles into town to see the dentist the next morning. To ensure his compliance with her wishes, his wife had already made an appointment for him.

Otis had no pain the following morning and told his wife so.

She, however, told him to get to the dentist that morning or she was going to pull out the tooth.

Otis got into his pickup and headed toward town.

About twenty miles from town, the tooth pain returned. By the time Otis arrived at the dentist's office, the toothache was worse than ever. Otis told the receptionist his toothache story. He admitted that he was glad he finally listened to his wife.

Following the dentist's office protocol, the young woman dental assistant transcribed a brief history about her patient's dental pain, his medications, any allergies, and any serious health problems.

Except for the toothache, Otis advised the young woman that he was healthy.

The dental assistant then took x-rays of Otis' teeth and asked him to wait for the dentist.

The dentist came in to see Otis a short time later. Otis reaffirmed for the dentist the history he had given to his dental assistant. The dentist examined Otis' mouth, looked at the x-rays, and reexamined the mouth.

By now, Otis said his toothache was getting really bad. He became sweaty because of the severe pain. The dentist told Otis that the pain could not be coming from his wisdom tooth because he had no wisdom teeth. He told Otis to wait until he found a doctor to see him.

I received a call from the dentist just before noon. He gave me his patient's history and his examination and x-ray findings. The dentist told me he thought Otis needed to be seen right away.

I asked the dentist to bring the man to my office, which was located only two blocks away.

I asked my nurse to defer her lunch break so we could care for a patient that was coming straight from the dentist's office. She agreed without hesitation.

The dental assistant arrived with Otis just a few minutes later. Otis appeared pale and sweaty. His pulse was weak and irregular. His blood pressure was only 90/60 lying down (pronounced 90 over 60. 120/80 is normal). His breathing was not compromised.

As my nurse attached an oxygen mask to Otis, I obtained an electrocardiogram (ECG), or heart wave tracing that revealed a pattern consistent with an acute myocardial infarction (a heart attack) and an irregular rhythm. While my nurse inserted an intravenous catheter (an IV) to give medications, I had my secretary call the hospital intensive care unit to arrange for a bed.

My nurse and I transferred Otis with a wheelchair and arrived in the ICU a short time later. Soon thereafter his heart rhythm converted into a ventricular fibrillation pattern, a rhythm disorder that is not compatible with life. The ICU nurse promptly administered three successive electrical shocks to Otis' heart. Fortunately, the heart rhythm stabilized after the shocks.

I had the nurse administer a medication intravenously to prevent further rhythm problems. While the ICU nurse started a bedside vigil with Otis, I called his wife to inform her of his situation.

She told me that Otis never complained of any chest pain. She wondered how the toothache could have been his heart.

Briefly, I counseled her that the classic symptoms of a heart attack included chest pains, sweating, and nausea. However, only about twenty percent of heart attack patients present this way. About twenty percent of patients, especially women, have no pain. The remaining patients may complain of having pain, pressure, or discomfort of some sort in various locations, including the jaw, the neck, and the arms. I informed her that being suspicious is the real key to making the diagnosis.

I told the woman that she and Otis owed a debt of gratitude to her dentist, not me, because he was the one who was suspicious. He knew Otis had a medical problem and knew what to do.

I called the dentist to inform him of his patient's eventful day. I congratulated him on a job well done.

Otis fared well after his heart attack and was well enough to finish his fall fieldwork before the first snowstorm.

# If It's Three, Let It Be

Natalie was a young teacher in her early twenties from the nearby community of Fairview, Montana, who came into the clinic late one summer day complaining that she had a really bad yeast infection. She told me that all of a sudden several days before she developed a severe itching in her genital area. Natalie told me she had never had a yeast infection, but after talking with some friends, she knew that was her problem. Unfortunately, the over-the-counter anti-yeast preparations she had used for the past two days did not work. Natalie said the itching had become almost unbearable.

When I asked Natalie about recent things she may have done differently regarding feminine hygiene, she reported that nothing had changed.

After my further inquiries regarding bathing, chemicals, sexual habits, etc., produced no positive answers, I asked Natalie if I could examine her genital area and test the stuff coming out of her.

She gave me her permission.

With my patient undressed on the examination table, I saw many blisters in a linear pattern on her lower legs, buttocks, and inner thighs. Some of the lines of blisters went up into her vagina. Her entire external genital area was swollen and covered with blisters and redness. Her vagina was a bed of blisters. The stuff coming out of her vagina was nothing more than the fluid from the ruptured blisters *inside* her vagina.

I tested the fluid for yeast and other common vaginal infection germs. All the test results were negative.

The skin eruption appeared like the allergic contact dermatitis caused by poison ivy, a common plant that grew in many areas in the valley. I relayed my thoughts to Natalie and asked if there was something else she had not told me.

Somewhat sheepishly Natalie mentioned that she met Claus.

I asked Natalie to tell me more about Claus.

Natalie told me that Claus Bjorken was one of the Danes who worked on one of the farms near Fairview. (The farmers in our area had recruited worker-students from Denmark for years. The young men usually had summer work visas. They learned about Montana agriculture practices while providing a needed work force for the host farmers.)

I asked Natalie to tell me more.

Natalie told me that she was embarrassed to talk about their encounter because she had never done anything like that before.

I assured her that I would not pass judgment on her personal activities. I just wanted to figure out her problem.

Reassured, Natalie told me that she had met Claus and his friends at the local pizza restaurant one evening. Since she was new to the area and did not know a lot about farming, Claus offered to teach her how to irrigate the sugar beet fields using siphon tubes. She agreed. Natalie met Claus early the next morning for work. Not only did she learn about irrigating fields, but also she learned about planting, weeding, and fertilizing sugar beets. By mid-afternoon all the irrigation tubes were set. The pair just had to wait a few hours before the tubes could be set again. They decided to take a walk down by the river.

Natalie explained that it was really hot outside. When Claus took off his shirt to cool off, she became sexually excited. After a pause, Natalie continued to tell me that, "One thing led to another," and, before too long, the pair was rolling around in the buff by the river.

Later, they put on their clothes and finished irrigating the fields.

I knew Natalie was hurting, but I just had to laugh. After a few moments, she laughed too.

I asked Natalie if she had a good time.

She said, "It was amazing!"

I knew that the oily substance produced by the poison ivy plant, called urushiol, is a profound allergen to most people. Its three narrow leaves on a stem identify the plant. The chemical reacts with the skin anywhere it touches causing an allergic reaction. After viewing the irritation pattern on Natalie, I had a good guess what happened in the bushes by the river that hot day.

I knew that the oil had to be removed from my patient's skin and vagina. Therefore, I gave Natalie instructions on how to make a slurry with baking soda and vinegar. I asked her to apply the concoction everywhere. Additionally, I prescribed an antihistamine and some oral cortisone tablets to be used until the itching resolved. Finally, I asked Natalie to wash all the clothes she wore that day and her bed linens to remove any chemical residue. I requested that Natalie telephone me the next day to tell me how she was doing.

The following morning, Natalie called to tell me that she was a lot better but not well yet. I knew she should be as good as new in a few weeks.

Late that afternoon, I had a walk-in patient named Claus Bjorsen from Copenhagen, Denmark. Claus complained of a severe rash and itching all over, especially on his groin and genitals.

I asked Claus only a few questions before prescribing treatments for his poison ivy. I already knew the story.

I did advise Claus to watch where he wandered down by the river, because poison ivy grew everywhere. I told him to remember the popular saying about poison ivy, *"If it's three, let it be."*

# Paying Bills

A storm arose during the night in the winter of 1978 that slowed travel around Sidney and all of northeastern Montana. The temperature hovered around zero degrees. The winds were substantial and made the wind chill about minus forty degrees or more. The snow came horizontally because of the wind. However, this was winter in Montana, and these weather events were expected. The entire clinic staff arrived for work on time except Doctor Smyth, my colleague in the clinic, who was stranded by an ice storm in western Montana.

The snow and wind intensified into a white out blizzard by mid morning. From my office window I could not see the hospital complex that was just across the street. The air was totally white, and the wind was howling.

Instead of managing the usual telephone calls to make appointments for patients, the receptionists and the nurses busied themselves with other tasks that needed tending around the clinic. The entire clinic calendar for the day was cancelled by noon, either by the patients calling in to cancel their appointments or by my office staff telephoning patients to warn them of the weather hazards.

About 10:30 a.m. the blizzard seemed to abate slightly. Our lab technician Tom suggested that instead of all the staff going out for lunch, we could have an early lunch. He would use his big four-wheel-drive truck and get some take-out food at a local restaurant called The Windmill that was about a half mile away. Tom had already called The Windmill and found out that they were still open for business during the storm.

I thought this was a grand idea. I informed the staff that lunch was on me. After collecting our orders, Tom left.

While Tom was gone, the remaining clinic staff members and I discussed closing the clinic for the day. It seemed obvious to me that no patients would be coming. Besides, I thought that the employees, some of whom lived miles out of town, needed to get home safely before dark or before the storm became worse. I knew that some of the employees might be concerned about a loss of pay for the hours they would lose. Therefore, I assured them that they would receive pay for the entire day.

Tom returned after an hour or so. When asked about the delay, he reported that the electric power went out and that he had no idea how they cooked our food. Tom handed each of us our order.

I had ordered a deluxe double cheeseburger, but my burger had no meat. I showed my staff how my deluxe hamburger was made with lettuce, tomatoes, pickles, and mustard, and, by the way, hold the burger.

The staff laughed as I consumed my original Sidney, Montana, veggie burger.

Just after noon and as the entire staff was at the front counter preparing to close the clinic doors, an elderly woman walked in. She was bundled up so that only her face could be seen. Her coat and hood were covered with snow. Her glasses became frosted as she entered the building. After the elderly woman had removed her hood and warmed her glasses so she could see, the clinic receptionist asked how she could help.

The elderly woman said, "I'm here to pay my bill."

My receptionist asked how she got to the clinic.

The woman replied, "I walked."

The receptionist asked her, "Why on earth did you come out in weather like this? You could have gotten hurt." After a short pause she added, "You could have waited until the weather cleared, you know?"

The woman proclaimed, "Today is my bill paying day. Besides, there are no cars on the streets. Walking is perfectly safe."

After the woman paid her clinic bill, Tom offered to escort her through the blizzard in his truck to finish her bill paying chores.

The elderly woman declined his generosity and reassured us that she would be just fine because she was a tough, old Norwegian. To the amazement of the entire staff, the woman then departed into the cold and whiteness of the winter storm to complete her monthly bill paying duties.

The clinic staff closed the doors and headed home in the blizzard.

The elderly Norwegian woman called the clinic the next morning to let us know she had a pleasant walk in the snow and arrived home safely.

# Rotation Cap

The nurse's notation on the new patient's chart outside the examination room read "painful rotation cap?" As I entered the examination room, I met Mr. Handley Merrill for the first time. This was the early spring of 1978. Mr. Merrill was a man in his late sixties who, I thought, looked eighty years old or more. Mr. Merrill had a farm-ranch operation about fifty miles from any town, and he liked it that way.

After I asked Mr. Merrill how I could help him that day, he told me, "My dad gum rotation cap is giving me fits. I think I need another one of them there cortisone shots right here." He then pointed toward a place in front of his left shoulder.

I asked Mr. Merrill to tell me more about his bad rotation cap.

Mr. Merrill explained that in his day he had been a pretty fair cowboy and rode saddle broncs and bulls on weekends "to make a livin." Since he was a lefty, Mr. Merrill held the ropes with his left hand. He told me, "All that fun took a terrible toll on my good arm, and my *rotation cap* just gave up."

I asked Mr. Merrill if he did not mean a *rotator cuff*.

He replied, "Yeh, whatever you doctors want to call it." He then went on to tell me that his shoulder "hurt somethin' fierce" at times. Lately, his shoulder pain had kept him awake at night. Mr. Merrill complained that he couldn't get his farm chores done.

I asked Mr. Merrill why he thought he needed a cortisone shot.

He explained that he had been receiving cortisone injections from an orthopedic surgeon in Billings for about five years. He usually got one before spring planting and during the harvest in the fall when he used his arm the most. He told me the orthopedist had given him a cortisone shot no more than a few weeks before, but it didn't seem to be working as well as usual. Mr. Merrill thought it was just too far to drive the two hundred fifty miles or so to Billings for a simple shot, so he came to see me. He told me that if I would just give him the shot, he'd be on his way back home.

I asked Mr. Merrill if I could examine his shoulder before I gave him a shot.

He agreed.

Upon examining the man's shoulders, I was unable to produce any physical findings that would suggest a rotator cuff problem. I told Mr. Merrill that his left shoulder seemed to be working fine without pain.

He replied, "Well, Doc, it hurts real good right now."

I asked Mr. Merrill if the orthopedic surgeon examined his shoulder before the injection several weeks before.

He told me, "Hell, no. He knows me too well for that. I told the nurse what I needed, and the doc gave it to me."

I asked Mr. Merrill to lie down on the examination table so I could examine him further.

With hesitation, he did as I asked. However, he commented to me that it might have been easier for him to drive to Billings after all.

My examination revealed only arthritic changes and stiffness at many joints and *a heart murmur.*

When I asked Mr. Merrill if he ever had rheumatic fever (a common childhood disease caused by a streptococcus bacterium that causes heart murmurs) or was ever told that he had a murmur, he told me that he didn't recall.

I told Mr. Merrill that I wanted to perform a heart test because of his heart murmur.

He said, "Doc, are you just trying to rip off an old ranch hand?"

After I reassured Mr. Merrill that I was not trying to rip him off, he consented to have an ECG (electrocardiogram).

While I tended to another clinic patient, my nurse came into the exam room to perform the test.

The ECG tracing had evidence for an acute inferior wall myocardial infarction (heart attack on the bottom of the heart). There was additional evidence on the tracing for enlargement of my patient's heart. However, I couldn't tell if the changes were old or new. I told Mr. Merrill that I thought he was having a heart attack, not rotator cuff arthritis, and that I needed to admit him to the hospital.

Mr. Merrill said, "The heck! I don't have no chest pain."

After spending a short time convincing Mr. Merrill of my concerns, he allowed me to admit him to the ICU with a possible heart attack. The morphine I gave Mr. Merrill for his *rotation cap* pain produced relief in moments.

Blood tests used to measure heart enzymes were completed a few hours later and confirmed my diagnosis of an acute myocardial infarction. Despite his reluctance, I persuaded Mr. Merrill to stay in the hospital.

Mr. Merrill had an uncomplicated course in the hospital. His cardiac rehabilitation afterward included working on his farm during planting season but with a lot less physical intensity. He recovered extremely well.

After this incident, I notified the orthopedic surgeon of my findings and about Mr. Merrill's heart disease.

Interestingly, until his death almost ten years later, Mr. Merrill required no more cortisone shots for his torn *rotation cap.*

# To Be and Not To Be

One summer's day in the clinic, my nurse put a note on the patient's chart outside an examination room that read, "REALLY needs to talk." (This kind of note usually meant that I was in for an extended session with the patient.) As I entered the room, I saw an attractive middle-aged woman who was wiping away tears with a tissue but who was not crying overtly. The woman's name was Lorraine Andrus. Soon after I introduced myself, Lorraine informed that she was in her mid-thirties, she had two teenage children, she and her husband wanted no more children, and she was pregnant! The longer Lorraine talked, the more visibly upset she became.

I asked Lorraine how I could help her.

She didn't know.

I sat on my examination stool waiting for this woman to compose herself. After a few minutes, Lorraine told me that she had been an advocate for the Right to Life organization for years. She did not want another child at her age, but having an abortion was not an option for her. Her husband, however, wanted her to have an abortion. This disagreement had caused friction between them.

Having had a similar experience while serving in the National Health Service Corps,[24] I empathized with Lorraine. However, I knew that something would happen with her pregnancy, one way or another. I gave Lorraine my usual talk about unwanted pregnancy choices. That is, the mother could either keep a pregnancy or not. If she decided to keep the pregnancy, she could either keep the baby or give it away. If she decided not to have the pregnancy, then I would assist her finding a clinic that performed pregnancy termination procedures. I did not perform the procedure. I told Lorraine that I would provide her assistance whatever she decided.

After an examination, I estimated that Lorraine's pregnancy was only six to eight weeks old, so I advised her that there was

---

[24] The National Health Service Corps or NHSC is a government program that has provided healthcare personnel to medical shortage areas in the United States since 1972. The program offers scholarships to some medical professionals to help repay their education loans.

some time to consider her options. Lorraine left the clinic with the understanding that she would inform me of her decision soon.

A week or so later, Lorraine returned to the clinic to inform me that she and her husband decided to keep their baby. My nurse and I informed Lorraine about the prenatal care our clinic provided. She elected to begin her prenatal care that day with me.

Lorraine returned to the clinic soon thereafter before her next scheduled appointment. The nurse's note on Lorraine's chart outside the exam room read "Needs to talk."

As I entered the room, Lorraine was tearful. Lorraine reminded me that she was a firm believer in the Right to Life philosophy. She believed that abortions, no matter what the reason, were wrong. She was carrying a baby that she had considered aborting, but she could not because of her beliefs. Now, however, the family had a situation at home. Their teenage daughter, their honor student high school kid, was pregnant. Lorraine told me that she needed some help.

I asked who needed the help.

Lorraine replied, "All of us."

I asked Lorraine how far along her daughter's pregnancy was.

She was unsure, but she figured it was perhaps two or three months.

Again, Lorraine and I talked about unwanted pregnancies. I suggested that I, or someone, be allowed to examine her daughter soon. Pregnancy terminations at the time were generally done before twelve weeks. Therefore, it became imperative to determine the age of the pregnancy before any referral was made, if that was the course of action the family wished to pursue.

Lorraine told me that she was too young when she had her daughter and that she did not want her daughter's life to be disrupted as her life had been. However, she cried saying something like, "I'm saving my own baby but wanting to kill my own grandchild. What is wrong with me?"

After taking a short time to regain her composure, Lorraine asked if she could bring her daughter into the office that day after school.

I told Lorraine we would make time to see her.

That afternoon, a pregnancy test confirmed the girl's pregnancy. I examined Lorraine's teenage daughter and found her to have an eight-week-size uterus. By now, both Lorraine and her daughter were weeping.

After my examination, I gave my unwanted pregnancy speech to the daughter. I told the mom and the daughter that they had some time to consider their options. As a precaution, however, I gave Lorraine the name and telephone number of a clinic that performed terminations along with my dated examination notes.

The pair thanked my nurse and me before they left.

At her next prenatal visit, Lorraine told me that her daughter had an abortion on the Friday after her clinic visit. Lorraine said she and her husband had some sleepless nights, but she now believed they made the correct decision. Lorraine admitted that she now had a different perspective on abortions.

I did not discuss this episode again with anyone.

Lorraine delivered a beautiful baby girl in the spring. Upon this girl's graduation from high school eighteen years later, my wife Kay and I gave Lorraine's daughter a scholarship for college from our Ashcraft Foundation program.

I had the good fortune to be this family's doctor for almost twenty-five years.

# Toasted

I met Jeremy for the first time in my office. He presented as a walk-in patient on a Tuesday morning after a Fourth of July holiday weekend. Jeremy was a well-tanned young man in his twenties who was wearing well-worn Levi jeans and a loose fitting long-sleeved shirt. I assumed he worked on a ranch. I noticed that Jeremy appeared to be restless and uncomfortable. After I introduced myself, I asked how I could assist him.

Jeremy said he was having a lot of pain and needed my help.

I told the young man that I would do what I could, and I asked him to tell me more about his problem.

Jeremy informed me that he worked on a ranch outside of town during the week and was a rodeo bull rider on weekends. He told me he had experienced injuries with considerable pain with his work, but nothing hurt quite like the pain he was having now.

I asked him to tell me more about his pain.

Jeremy replied, "Doc, I'll just show ya." At that moment he took off his shirt and said, "Do you see my problem?"

Jeremy had redness and numerous small intact blisters over his entire back and part of his chest.

I told the young man he had a really bad sunburn. I asked him how he could let it get so bad.

Jeremy told me he had participated in a rodeo on Friday and Saturday. Afterward, he and his girlfriend spent the weekend water skiing on the Fort Peck reservoir with some friends. After water skiing the next two days in the full sun, they could barely move Monday night. Not only did they have sore muscles, but also they had really bad sunburn pain. Jeremy told me that he and his girlfriend tried to soothe their skin with vinegar, cool water compresses, and Tylenol. However, the sunburn pain did not subside. The pain intensified so much that neither of them could sleep. Finally, they packed up early that morning and drove the one hundred forty miles from Fort Peck Lake to Sidney to seek medical attention.

As I was about to ask Jeremy another question, he said, "Hold on, Doc. You ain't seen nothin' yet." He then carefully removed his boots and his pants to reveal more redness and a few small blisters on his legs. There was a distinct line delineating where his swimming suit had been.

I told him that I could see why he was in pain.

Jeremy, now in anguish, grunted with, "Hey, Doc, that's not the half of it. Here's where the *real pain* is." He then removed his underwear to reveal his genital and anal areas that were covered with blisters too.

I was impressed with this sunburn. Certainly, it was the most severe that I had seen.

Anticipating my next question, Jeremy said, "My girl and me were in a secluded part of the lake, so we decided to ski in the buff the second day. Wasn't too smart, was it?"

When I commented to Jeremy that sunlight reflecting off the water amplifies the effects of the sun and increases the chances of getting sunburned, he said jokingly, "Now you tell me. My manhood may never be the same."

I asked Jeremy if he brought his girlfriend with him.

He told me that Amber, his girlfriend, was in the waiting room. He offered to bring her back to the examination room.

I asked Jeremy to sit still, and I had my office assistant escort Amber back to the examination room.

I waited outside Jeremy's room to watch for his girlfriend. As my nurse escorted Amber around a corner, I could see that she was walking bowlegged wearing a loose dress and sandals. Amber had red hair, a fair complexion, and a bright red face and arms covered with blisters. After I greeted Amber, I had her enter the examination room to be with Jeremy.

I relayed Jeremy's story to Amber. She confirmed the essentials of the tale.

When I asked Amber if I could evaluate her sunburn, she said that she was embarrassed and that she was not wearing underwear.

Jeremy quipped, "I'm not either!"

After Amber gave me her consent for an examination, I summoned my nurse to take Amber into another room. After she was in a gown, my nurse and I evaluated Amber's sunburn. Because of her fair complexion, Amber had more blistering. Additionally, her genital area was raw and excoriated along with many ruptured blisters.

When I relayed my observations to Amber, she said that they had sex on the beach *before* they started to hurt so badly. That night, however, the pain in her genital area was excruciating. Now crying, Amber told us that the pain was almost unbearable.

My nurse reunited the pair in an examination room. I told the pair that they, unfortunately, were going to get worse before they got better. Both of them had severe second-degree burns and had the potential for dehydration, infection, and other things. I suggested that I would like to place them in the hospital for a few days.

They declined noting that neither of them had health insurance.

Since the pair was living in the same apartment, I told them that they could be each other's nurses for the next ten days. I asked each of them to drink at least two gallons of fluid a day to prevent dehydration. My nurse and I showed them how to apply occlusive dressings to the areas where the blisters had broken. I gave them a large jar of Silvadene cream, a commonly used product for burns, and demonstrated how it should be applied several times a day. I wrote each patient a prescription for pain medication. Finally, I asked Jeremy and Amber to keep a written log of everything they drank, every time they urinated, and their temperatures four times a day.

Looking at me tearfully, Amber asked me if they were going to die.

I told her that I didn't think so if they took care of themselves. I told the pair that I would call on them at their apartment daily until I thought they were better.

They agreed.

I examined Jeremy's and Amber's burns daily at their home for about a week until their burns were no longer weeping and new skin had started to cover the wounds.

The pair turned out to be pretty good nurses for each other.

I knew that these young people had little money and no insurance, so I never sent them a bill.

The pair married about a year later. Over the next few years, I had the privilege of assisting Amber during the birth of their two children.

# Hair Day

Late one Wednesday evening in 1977, a pregnant woman came to our hospital in labor with her first child. Assuming the birthing process progressed normally, I knew that a woman's first labor took about sixteen to twenty hours on average. Therefore, I estimated that my patient would have her baby born about noon the next day.

About 9 a.m., my patient's uterine cervix was dilated to five centimeters (ten centimeters is fully dilated). If all went well, I anticipated that my patient should have her baby in about two to three hours, or about noon.

Unfortunately, despite a good labor pattern with strong contractions, the baby stopped moving down the birth canal. After several more hours of vigorous labor, the cervix did not dilate past five centimeters. Because this was the woman's first pregnancy, she was not tired, and the baby showed no signs of distress, I allowed her to continue to labor. The obstetrics nurse and I, however, watched closely for any signs of distress, either from our mom-to-be or from her unborn baby.

About noon, the mom's cervix was still five centimeters dilated, and the baby's head had not budged in 3 hours. The mom had become fatigued. I knew it was time to perform a Cesarean section. After discussing the situation with the mother and her husband, I asked the OB nurse to prepare the mom for an operation. Then, I walked to the operating room, which was just a short distance away in our small hospital, to inform the surgical team that I wanted to perform an urgent C-section.

Upon entering the surgical area, I met Jasmine Bertrand, the operating room supervisor. When I advised Mrs. Bertrand of my obstetrics patient's failure to progress in labor and that she would require a C-section as soon as the team could get ready, she stared at me and said, "I don't think so."

Taken aback by her comment, I asked what she meant.

Mrs. Bertrand repeated in a stern voice, "I don't think we can do an operation this afternoon."

I asked why the surgery could not be done.

She replied, "Because I have my hair done every Thursday afternoon! Everybody knows that!"

Shocked and bewildered by a nurse who would put her hair appointment above the needs of a patient, I responded with, "I really don't care about your hair. I do care about my pregnant mom who's in trouble. If you are not willing to help, then I will do it by myself." I then went into the operating room and started to unwrap our emergency C-section supplies and instruments.

Within a few moments, Mrs. Bertrand walked to the door of the operating room and, after letting out a big sigh, told me that they would be ready in five minutes.

I looked at Jasmine and said sarcastically, "Thank you." I continued on to the obstetrics area to see my patient.

Along with Mrs. Bertrand working as the surgical scrub nurse, I performed the C-section and retrieved a healthy female baby without a problem. When I assured myself that the baby was stable, I handed her to the nurse from the nursery who was waiting in the operating room by the infant warmer.

When I asked Jasmine for a needle holder so I could suture the mother's wounds, she informed me that the instrument was contaminated when the OB pack was opened. However, it was in the sterilizer and would be ready soon. Jasmine and I waited a few minutes for the instrument to arrive. The circulator nurse brought in the needle holder and dropped it onto the sterile surgical drapes where Jasmine picked it up. Promptly, she slapped the instrument, which was still extremely hot from being in the sterilizer, onto my outstretched palm.

I glared at Jasmine.

She glared back at me.

I didn't say a word.

The remainder of the operation went well. The mom and baby were taken back to their respective rooms in stable condition. Afterward, I changed my clothes and went to my office.

Soon thereafter, I learned that Jasmine *always* took Thursday afternoons off for a hair appointment. Instead of discussing this incident with the hospital administrator, I made sure that I planned an *emergency* operation for hair day afternoons for a few weeks. When Jasmine changed her hair day, I changed my afternoon surgeries to coincide.

This little power struggle lasted about a month or two before Jasmine cornered me in the Doctor's lounge after a morning of surgical cases. She asked me when she could schedule a hair appointment during the week. Jasmine told me that she did not get her hair done on the weekends.

I informed her that she could schedule her hair day anytime she wanted as long as she was always available for emergencies.

Jasmine concurred.

Jasmine's hair day was not discussed again.

# Pitch Black

Agnes, a woman in her late seventies, was a widow who lived alone in town. Late one afternoon, she felt ill and walked about eight blocks from her home to our hospital's emergency room. After performing her initial evaluation, the emergency room nurse summoned me to see Agnes who was complaining of abdominal pains.

Upon my arrival in the emergency room, I noticed that Agnes was lying still on a bed and did not appear to be in any acute distress. Looking at the emergency room form, I noticed that her vital signs were normal.

When I questioned Agnes about her abdominal pain, she would tell me only that she didn't feel good, and her belly hurt. She denied having fevers, chills, nausea, vomiting, or diarrhea. Agnes told me that she had been eating "just fine." Agnes denied having previous episodes that were similar to this one and told me that she had been healthy all her life.

My visual examination of Agnes revealed numerous surgical scars on her abdomen. Despite being healthy, Agnes had incurred surgeries to remove her appendix, gallbladder, ovaries, and uterus. In addition, Agnes admitted having other surgeries for stomach ulcers, abdominal adhesions, varicose veins, a thyroid goiter, and some bowel problem. Agnes seemed quite proud of herself to have endured so many surgeries.

I thought to myself, "There are many good reasons that would explain this woman's bellyache."

Except for some mild upper abdominal tenderness, my examination of Agnes did not reveal any acute, life-threatening process. However, considering my patient's age and her surgical history, I decided it best to observe Agnes in the hospital overnight.

Looking at the nursing notes in Agnes' chart the next morning, I saw that the night nurse had written, "0300, Patient had a large, black, tarry stool. Patient comfortable at 0330." There was no documentation of a guaiac test being performed on the stool (This test confirms the presence of blood. Also called a fecal occult blood test).

Knowing that a black, tarry stool suggested blood in the bowel, I asked the dayshift supervisor if the night nurse had commented on her findings, or if the night nurse had performed a guaiac test on the black, tarry stool and forgotten to record the results.

The day shift supervisor told me that nothing was mentioned during their morning report.

I obtained the materials to perform a guaiac test on my patient's stool and headed to her room. Unfortunately, with my examination, I found no fecal material in my patient's rectum to test for blood. In addition, Agnes felt fine and wanted to go home.

Because of the night nurse's notations in the chart, I felt obligated to continue watching Agnes and, perhaps, to perform more invasive testing to look for pathology in her intestines. After I explained my dilemma to Agnes, she agreed to stay in the hospital another day.

I happened to be in the hospital for another hospital admission during the early morning hours the next day. While I was at the nursing work station writing orders for my new patient, I saw the night nurse who had recorded the "black, tarry stools" the previous day on Agnes' chart. A short time later when she came out from Agnes' room, I asked the nurse about the "black, tarry stool" she had seen and if she had done a guaiac test on the sample.

The nurse, who was experienced and nearing retirement, asked me, "Doctor, what is a guaiac test?"

After I explained to the nurse about the test, she told me that she had never done one.

I thought everyone knew about the guaiac test. It had been a standard procedure when checking for occult blood in feces for almost fifty years.

The nurse then said, "Agnes, just went to the toilet. Doctor, would you show me how to do the test?"

I agreed.

The nurse went into my patient's bathroom before me. Before I entered, I asked the nurse what she saw.

She said, "Doctor, there is another black stool."

When I entered the bathroom, the light was off, and the nurse was staring into the toilet. I asked her how she could see anything in the dark.

The nurse told me that, over the years, she "had learned to see quite well in the dark."

I told the nurse that I could not see into the toilet in the dark and asked her to turn on the bathroom light.

The aging nurse replied, "No, Doctor, you'll wake up my patients. They need their rest." The nurse pulled out her small pocket flashlight that, when turned on and pointed into the toilet, illuminated a brown piece of stool.

I retrieved a small sample of the fecal material from the toilet bowel. I then led the nurse outside the dark patient room into the lighted hallway to demonstrate for her how to perform a guaiac test.

Fortunately for Agnes, the test was negative for blood.

Afterward, I suggested to the nurse that the next time she saw a black, tarry stool in a toilet, she should confirm her observation *with the lights on,* and she should test the stool for blood.

The aging nurse retired a few months later. She said nursing care was becoming too technical.

# Echo Boomers

He who teaches children learns more than they do.

German proverb

# Royalty

Miserable winter weather was common for northeastern Montana in the late 1970s and 1980s. Outside a blizzard had raged all day. The wind chill temperatures approached minus thirty degrees Fahrenheit. The airport was closed. The roads were closed, and no travel was permitted. Because of the blizzard outside, I had decided earlier in the day to spend the night in the hospital just in case an emergency occurred. Into the emergency room in the darkness of late afternoon entered a pregnant woman in labor accompanied by her husband. Since I was in the hospital, I was called to attend to this woman.

I learned that the pair came from the eastern United States, and he worked in the oil fields. They had been in our area for a short time. Additionally, she had not seen anyone for her prenatal care in the past two months because of their moving around. Fortunately, the woman had her medical records from her obstetrician. (With the terrible weather, I certainly did not want to call in the laboratory technicians to run blood tests if it was not absolutely necessary.)

During a short period of introductions, I ascertained that this was the woman's first pregnancy. Her medical records revealed nothing abnormal. She was near her estimated due date, and by observing her body language, I knew she was in labor.

The nurse and I continued to evaluate the woman. Her labor was regular with appropriate intervals between the contractions. The fetal heart tones were normal and did not vary appreciably with the contractions. My examination of her pelvis revealed a cervix that was soft and four centimeters dilated. After a short discussion with the parents-to-be about my findings and my thoughts, I transferred the woman from the emergency room to the obstetrics wing of the hospital.

A short time later, several friends came to visit the woman and her husband. Why they would risk going out in the horrendous weather would be made clear to me later. For now, however, they were just supportive friends as far as I knew.

The woman's labor progressed unremarkably. When the time came for her to be transferred to the delivery suite, she asked me if her friends could be allowed to come too. I told the friends that I had no objection as long as they behaved themselves.

They promised.

In the delivery room, the woman pushed hard for what seemed a long time. I knew that this was her first pregnancy, and her pelvis was very tight at the outlet. When the baby's heart tones started to drop significantly with each contraction, I injected an anesthetic to anesthetize the woman's entire bottom. I then applied forceps to the baby's head. With the mother pushing steadily and firmly with each contraction, I assisted the baby out with firm traction on the forceps. The baby came out floppy and stunned.

As I was suctioning the newborn's mouth and nose and wiping its face, the new mom asked me what kind of baby she had.

I had not looked yet because I had been busy dealing with a stunned baby. I peered between the baby's legs and told the mom that she had a girl.

The new father asked me, "Would you please repeat that?"

I told the couple again they had a baby girl.

The father then yelled out, "Hallelujah! It's a girl! Honey, we have a girl! Can you believe it?"

The new mom just smiled at her husband. She asked me, "Doctor, how is my daughter. She isn't crying very loud."

I told her, "She's a little bit pokey, but she's breathing just fine."

When the baby started to cry vigorously, I heard the father say, "We have a girl! We have a daughter!' He was almost overcome with joy. I had never seen a display in the delivery room quite like this one.

I looked up to check on the friends who had been standing outside the delivery room. The nurse said they went to find a telephone. (This was before cell phones. Phones were connected to real wires back then.)

I placed the baby next to the new mom who was crying with joy. Dad was crying too. The nurse was so caught up in the excitement of the moment that she too was crying.

The remainder of the delivery process was unremarkable. Afterward, the mom went back to her room, and the newborn went to the nursery for observation. It was now some time in the early hours of the morning; I went to the doctor's lounge to take a nap.

The next morning the skies had cleared, and the sun was shining. The blizzard had passed leaving high snowdrifts everywhere, but the outside temperature remained well below zero. A large group of people standing in front of the nursery window greeted me as I walked by. I was given a dozen cigars. I asked the nurse, "Where did they come from?"

She replied, "They all showed up about six this morning."

The new mom and dad greeted me as I entered the room. There must have been twenty pots or bouquets of flowers adorning the room. She asked, "Can you believe this?" as she pointed to all the flowers.

I had to admit the sight was impressive. I mentioned to the mom that somebody must think a lot of her.

The woman replied with a big smile, "It's not me. It's her!" She pointed toward about ten Polaroid photographs her friends had taken of the newborn that morning. "She's very special."

I told her that I thought all babies are special.

The new dad inserted, "Doc, you don't know the half the story. This is the first girl born into my family in three generations. She's not just a special baby girl. She's a baby princess. Just wait until tomorrow!"

When I asked about what was going to happen tomorrow, the dad said, "You'll see."

That evening during my rounds I asked the nurse on duty how her day went. She told me that flowers and cards had been coming in all day for the baby princess. Otherwise, all my patients fared well during the day. My new mom's first attempts at nursing her baby went well.

The new mom asked me, "Is this amazing or what?" as she pointed to many more flowers. The nurses had to open up the adjacent OB room just for flowers and gifts. The OB wing smelled like a floral shop. The woman told me that the families in the East were chartering an airplane to bring them to see her baby, and her husband went out with their friends to celebrate.

The following day an entourage of about twenty people poured into the hospital to see the new princess. One of the entourage asked me when the mom could go home. The family planned to stay until that time and fly the entire family back East to visit the rest of the clan.

This was oil boom time in Sidney, Montana. Rooms rented *by the hour*. I had no idea where these people would find places to stay, but it did not seem to matter. After sixty years, these folks finally had a baby girl in the family.

I kept the mom and baby girl two days longer than usual just to allow them some time to rest.

Upon leaving the hospital, I wished the new mom and dad well. I had a feeling their lives were going to be privileged, and busy, for some time to come with a princess in the family.

# A Dead Cat

Esther came to the office one fall afternoon to ask me some questions about her husband who had recently been discharged from the hospital. Esther brought along Isabella, her three-year-old granddaughter since everyone else on the ranch was busy with the many jobs during the fall, and someone needed to watch the youngster.

After greeting Esther and Isabella in the examination room, Esther told me she had some questions to ask about Marvin, her husband. Esther said Marvin had emergency heart surgery in Billings the week before when they were visiting friends. The doctors gave her a list of instructions and medicines to discuss with me. Esther then started to rummage through a massive handbag looking for the elusive documents.

As grandma was digging through her bag, I noticed that Isabella had a variety of bruises of different colors on her arms and face. In addition, the little girl was missing her front teeth, and I knew it was far too early for the teeth to have fallen out naturally. I instinctively asked Isabella what happened to her teeth.

The youngster responded with, "They fell out in the barn."

I said to Isabella, "It makes you talk funny, doesn't it?"

She countered with, "Yeh."

Grandma chimed in, "The darn kid fell out of the hay loft where she wasn't supposed to be. She's a real tomboy. She's sure been a handful for her folks."

Then Isabella blurted out, "Our kitty died."

While still looking for the messages in her bag, Esther said, "I know that envelope is in here somewhere." Without looking up, Esther added, "Isabella found him dead in the barn yesterday morning."

I looked at Isabella and told her I was sorry to hear that her kitty had died. I asked her to tell me the kitty's name.

"Tom," she replied.

Esther finally found the elusive packet of papers. She continued to open a large manila envelope and began sifting through the many pieces of paper that it contained.

Not to be distracted, Isabella interrupted and asked me, "Do you know how I know'd he was dead?"

I responded, "No, I don't know. How did you know that Tom was dead?"

Isabella got excited and replied, "I pissed in his ear!"

Grandma immediately stopped what she was doing and exhorted, "Isabella Marie! What have I told you about telling stories?"

Taken aback, the child reared back her head and asked, "Wha?" (what)

Grandma Esther countered with, "You heard me young lady! Just stop it, right now! Just wait 'till we get home, and I'm going to wash your mouth out with soap!"

The little girl seemed to be confused and mad at the same time. She looked at her grandma with tears welling up in her eyes and asked, "Wha?" (what)

Esther got right up close to Isabella's face and exclaimed, "You know very well what I mean young lady! So just ZIP IT!"

Isabella started to wail and shed tears. She cried out, "Grandma, you don't love me anymore!"

I now had a concerned and frustrated woman because of the medical problems with her husband, which I had not even addressed yet, and a grandchild who was giving her fits. I had a screaming three-year-old girl who looked beat up, talked funny because of her missing front teeth, and feared bad things were going to happen to her once she got home. I was witnessing quite a show in my exam room, and I still had not seen Esther's pile of papers from the doctors in Billings. Perhaps as a reflex I asked Isabella if she could tell me more about her cat.

This comment got the little girl's attention. She replied, "Tom died, and I know'd he died, 'cause he din't move when I pissed in his ear."

Grandma Esther promptly interjected, "Little girl, I'm warning you!"

Isabella looked at me with her tear filled eyes and said, "I show you."

I said, "Okay."

Grandma then told me, "Doctor Ashcraft, you are not helping."

Before I could say another word, Isabella was pointing to the floor. She just said, "Down here" as if she wanted me to sit on the floor.

As I started to get off my examination stool to sit on the floor, Esther said, "Doctor, you're just making things worse!"

After I was seated on the floor, Isabella motioned for me to lie down, and then she squatted next to my head. I started to wonder what I had gotten myself into this time.

The little girl then leaned over my head, put her teary face next to my right ear, and gave me a slobbery wet "**psssst.**"

I was surprised. I was expecting something much worse. I moved to get up and started to laugh.

Isabella then stated, "You moved Doctor Jimmie when I **pissst** in your ear. Tom din't, so I know'd he was dead."

I looked at the grandmother and just started to laugh. A toothless three-year-old had gotten the best of us.

Esther smiled too. She also located her husband's papers.

Now, I could answer some questions about Grandpa Marvin.

# Aim Higher

The chart outside the examination room was for Cassandra Mason. A note attached to the chart read, "Needs to Talk." This was my nurse's way of forewarning me that a long counseling session may be facing me behind the closed door. As I entered the examination room, I introduced myself to my new patient.

The attractive young woman said, "Hello, Doctor Ashcraft, my name is Cassandra Mason. I was told that you know a lot about children. I could use your help." At this point the young woman became quite distraught, started to cry, and exclaimed, "I am a terrible teacher!"

After Miss Mason had a chance to regain her composure, I asked her to give me just a bit more information about her problem.

Miss Mason informed me that she was the new teacher at a country school about twenty miles from town. She had graduated from college with honors the previous spring, and this was her first teaching job.

I asked her why she thought she was a terrible teacher.

Miss Mason told me that she was having trouble with student discipline in her classroom.

Knowing that Miss Mason taught in a one-room school in the country with multiple grades, I asked if she had trouble with all the children or just a few.

She replied, "The boys! Especially the little boys!" She then continued to tell me about an incident that occurred in the school several days before. She told me that some of the first and second grade girls came up to her on the playground during recess and told her that some boys were making a mess in the bathroom. Miss Mason said she went to the boys' toilet and heard yelling and commotion inside. From behind the door she asked the boys what they were doing, but they paid no attention to her. She demanded that they come outside that instant, but the commotion inside the bathroom persisted. She did not know what to do. She knew she couldn't just barge into the boys' bathroom!

This young teacher then told me that her single-parent mother raised her and her sister. She had no real experience with boys, especially little ones. The only thing she knew about child development was what she had learned in college.

The noise and yelling persisted in the bathroom. Miss Mason knew she had to stop whatever was a going on. Miss Mason told me that she took a deep breath and barged into the boy's bathroom. To her shock and dismay, she found four little boys having a grand time. They were seeing who could come closest to urinating on the light fixture above them. There was urine all over the floor, but the little boys did not care.

I asked Miss Mason what she thought about this.

She replied, "If I were a better teacher, it never would have happened. Why on earth would anyone try to pee on a light on the ceiling?"

I answered, "Because they are little boys, and they could."

Then I laughed. I told her that it was just a contest. It had nothing to do with her. I asked her about the shenanigans the girls were pulling while she was in the boy's toilet.

The young woman thought a moment, and then said, "Now that you mention it, the girls were giggly that afternoon in class. I wonder what they were up to?"

I reminded Cassandra to recall her days as a child and if she ever did anything foolish or silly. I suggested to her that the actions of her students may not be a reflection upon her but rather their parents. Finally, I suggested that the kids needed to know, in my view, that there would be consequences for their actions, no matter their ages.

When Miss Mason left the office I was not sure I had helped her, but at least she was not crying. I was that someone who got to share her frustration.

A few days later, Miss Mason telephoned me. She told me that the little girls thought it was fun to pull down their panties and pee in the field while she was busy with the boys in the toilet.

Miss Mason decided to punish *all* the students, young and old, by having them spend their recess time the next week mopping and cleaning the toilets everyday. She showed the kids that she was the boss.

I never was told who shot the highest or if they hit the light.

# Hooked on Phonics

About 4:30 one summer afternoon, Marilyn came to my office to pay her bill and to discuss the status of her seventy-year-old grandmother who had become progressively forgetful while living out on the ranch. The family was considering their options, including placing the family matriarch into the local nursing home. I knew this was a tough time for all families as they tried to contend with the difficulties associated with aging.

Today, Marilyn's three-year-old daughter Brittany accompanied her. Marilyn informed me that she had picked up Brittany at a local childcare center. The young mom brought her daughter into town twice a week so she could be around other children her age, a luxury not found forty miles out in the country. Marilyn informed me that Brittany had gone on a field trip that day.

I asked the little girl where she went on her field trip.

She replied, "The libary."

I asked what she did at the library.

Brittany's reply was, "I saw books. And, I colored!"

I told Brittany that it sounded like she had a good time at the library.

Brittany's eyes became wide open, and she exclaimed, "I saw aminals!

"Wow!" I replied. "What animals did you see?"

The youngster immediately responded with, "A frickin line!"

With this statement, Marilyn sat up in her chair and was obviously startled by what had just come out of her little girl's mouth.

Instinctively I asked another question. I asked Brittany if she saw any other animals at the library.

The youngster gazed toward the ceiling, put her right hand on the right side of her jaw with her index finger pointed toward her temple, and said, "A frickin geraf!" After a short pause, she added excitedly, "A frickin zeba too!"

I probably looked astonished. I know the mother did.

Marilyn looked at me and said, "Doctor Ashcraft, I apologize for my daughter. I don't know what's gotten into her. I'm going to have to talk with her father. Sometimes he uses that kind of language when he is talking to the cows on the ranch. Maybe she picked it up from him. I just don't know."

Brittany had more to say to me about her library experience. She looked at her mom, then me, and asked, "Ya know my favortist aminal?"

I shook my head side to side as if to say no.

The little girl got excited again and said, "Show ya!" With that comment she started to rummage through her backpack.

As she looked for something in her backpack, the mother again offered me her apology.

I told her that no apology was needed.

By now Brittany had located the item she wanted and extracted it from her backpack. She said, "Here. A frickin elfant!"

She then presented to me a page from a coloring book that she had colored just for me at the library. At the bottom of the page was the name of the book, The Animals of Africa. The animal had a gorgeous three-year-old coloring job with a blue head, orange ears, a brown body, black feet, and a bright red trunk. Underneath the picture in bold letters was the name AFRICAN ELEPHANT. (a frickin elfant)

This girl was HOOKED ON PHONICS.

I said, "What a nice picture. It's a beautiful African elephant!"

Brittany quickly pointed out, "That what I say!"

Marilyn and I just smiled at each other.

Marilyn gave her daughter a big hug.

I put the picture on the wall in my office along with my other treasures from kids.

Marilyn and I went on to discuss her aging grandparent's situation while Brittany beamed at her pictures on my office wall.

# Sex Education

After I had been in practice for several years, the high school home economics teacher asked me if I would be interested in helping her with the sex education and the child development portion of her curriculum. She asked me to make presentations to the girls in her classes.

I agreed.

When I arrived for my first lecture, I noticed that the students were having a good time in the back of the classroom. They were playing with the newborn baby of one of their classmates! I knew that these girls already knew the basic facts of life without a sex education class.

After the class, I suggested to the teacher that the more appropriate time to provide sex education was *before* the girls became pregnant, not after. Therefore, sex education, in my opinion, should be started in the lower elementary grades.

She agreed.

I continued to give presentations to the high school home economics classes over the next several years. One year I provided obstetrical care for sixteen high school girls living within thirty miles of Sidney. My prior efforts to provide sex education to younger students met with considerable resistance from every direction, including the parents.

In my continuing effort to offer a more comprehensive sex education program in the school system, I went to a school board meeting one spring with the hope that the school board would allow an expansion of the sex education curriculum into the elementary schools. One of the male board members turned around in his chair, looked me in the eye, and proudly stated, "I learned sex ed in the back of a 1948 Chevy! It worked fine for me!" He then turned around and ignored me. My request was denied, again.

Interestingly, the following year all the sixth grade teachers requested that I present a sex education program to their students in the spring. This program would replace the sessions that I had been giving to the high school students. The home economics and physical education teachers would again teach the high school classes.

My first presentations were given to the sixth grade classes at the Westside Elementary School. The girls had one presentation, and the boys had another. I thought my presentations were simple, to the point, and at the appropriate level for sixth-grade children. On the blackboard, I drew simple pictures of the female and male reproductive systems *in color*!

Nearing the end of my talk to the boys, I was impressed with how well things had gone and how much the boys seemed to understand what I was saying.

Before I concluded the session, I asked for questions and/or comments from the kids. One youngster started to wave his arms vigorously and called out, "Teacher Doctor, you're wrong!"

I asked him, "What did I say that's not right?"

While pointing at my drawings, he replied, "Those things are NOT testicles! My mommy says those are my *family jewels*! My daddy says they are my *Rocky Mountain oysters*!"

I was amused. The other children laughed.

Before I could comment, the boy pointed at the blackboard and exclaimed, "And that is not a penis! It's a *peedee wacker*!"

# What am I worth?

Late one August day, a young couple came to the clinic to get tetanus boosters. They brought with them their little boy Tyler who was about four years old. The father had been working with his animals in the barns at the county fair and had stepped on a nail. Since he needed to have a tetanus booster, his wife decided to have her tetanus booster at the same time.

The couple's three older children remained at the fairgrounds with their farm animals, which included sheep, pigs, and market steers. The kids, like most farm and ranch children in the area, were active in their county 4-H programs and had raised their own animals to show off and sell at the annual livestock auction at the fair.

The entire family had spent most of their time at this year's fair caring for, weighing, measuring, and evaluating the children's animals in preparation for the annual auction. The dad stepped on the nail just after the last animal bidding of the day.

As my nurse was administering a tetanus injection to the father, the young boy asked me, "How many 'el bees' am I?"

I asked, "What are *el bees?*"

The dad explained to me that his son was watching the judge weigh his other childrens' farm animals. His son had asked the judge what the letters meant by what he wrote down.

The judge told the boy that the letters "lbs" (el bees) showed how much the animals weighed. His brother's steer weighed 1,020 "el bees."

The boy apparently had been talking about "el bees" all day.

After administering the two tetanus shots, my nurse looked at the little boy and said, "Well, Mister, let's see how many 'el bees' you are." She then pointed to the nearby scale.

The youngster readily hopped onto the scale.

After he settled down on the scale, my nurse adjusted the double arm balance and said, "Thirty-six pounds, I mean thirty-six 'el bees'."

Tyler hopped down and asked his mom, "How much am I?"

The mother promptly picked up her little boy and said, "At seventy-six cents per pound and thirty-six pounds, **I'd say you're priceless!**"

She then put her little boy down.

Tyler put his hands on his hips, strutted around a bit, and said, "I knew it!"

The adults all had a good laugh.

From that day forward, I would frequently ask kids how many "el bees" they were.

# Doctor, We Need You

Have a heart that never hardens,
and a temper that never tires,
and a touch that never hurts

Charles Dickens

# Billy Bob

I was walking around our nursing home's dementia ward (now called the Alzheimer's wing) looking for one of my elderly patients who had wandered away from her room. The nurse informed me that my patient's wandering was becoming more prevalent and that I should consider placing an escape alarm[25] on her.

I entered a room with two beds. One bed had an elderly woman who appeared asleep. The other bed was empty. As I walked to the center of the room, the person in the bed said, "Is that you?"

I paid little attention since the person was not the patient I was seeking. The petite elderly woman sat up on the side of her bed, looked curiously at me, and said, "Billy Bob, is that you?"

The nurse intervened and told the woman, "No Mable, this is Doctor Ashcraft."

Either not hearing the nurse or ignoring her, the elderly woman literally hopped out of bed, leaped at me, grabbed me firmly about my waist, and exclaimed, "Billy Bob! Billy Bob Johnson! It is you!" The woman then grasped my arm and started to lead me toward her bed.

The nurse tried to intervene, but Mable was not to be denied. She was going to talk with Billy Bob.

I sat next to Mable on the side of her bed. She said she had so much to tell me. She wanted to know how things were with the family in West Virginia. She wanted to tell me about her kids and her husband. She obviously had a lot to say to someone about something. She told me that we should sit down "like old times and talk for hours."

I looked to the awaiting nurse for help who was obviously getting a big kick out of my situation with this demented woman. However, she told Mable that it was almost time for lunch, and she needed to get dressed to be presentable at the table.

---

[25] An escape alarm is a small device that is attached to a patient. When the device passes a sensor on a doorway, an alarm sounds to alert the professional caregivers at the facility. The device is often used with nursing home patients who tend to wander aimlessly.

Mable looked at the nurse, looked at me, and then crawled back into bed.

The next day I related this encounter to the local surgeon and the scrub nurse while I was assisting with a vascular procedure. The surgeon noted that I should be nicknamed Billy Bob from now on.

Later in the operation, the surgeon needed some blood vessel ligatures called vesi-loops, which are nothing more than colored rubber bands. Red ones are used to constrict small arteries while blue ones are used on veins. The surgeon also knew that we had a new operating room circulator, the person who brings needed materials and instruments to the sterile surgical area. On this day, he decided to call vesi-loops, "Billy Bobs."

The surgeon called out, "Diana, we need some red Billy Bobs STAT!"

The young woman started off to the supply room in haste to find the Billy Bobs. She returned a few minutes later and asked the scrub nurse, "Where do I find them?"

Playing along with the gag, the scrub nurse said calmly, "I believe you will find them on the top shelf way in the back." (This was the actual location of the vesi-loops.)

The young technician went away to look as our surgical trio snickered under our masks. She returned to tell us that she could not find any red Billy Bobs. She would make sure that they were ordered ASAP.

Feigning frustration, the surgeon then said, "Well get me some blue Billy Bobs. We need them now!"

Diana was off again looking for the elusive blue Billy Bobs. Again, we giggled under our masks.

The circulator returned a bit later showing total frustration. She said there were no Billy Bobs to be found anywhere.

Finally, the surgeon asked Diana is she was any good at finding skyhooks.

Diana looked confused for a few moments before she realized she had been fooled. The surgical nurse told Diana what we really needed and exactly where to find them. Besides, we had been using them the entire operation.

I related these two stories to my office staff who found them amusing.

At Christmas time, my staff gave me a new sweatshirt as a gift. The front was imprinted with large, bold letters — ***Billy Bob!***

I wore the sweatshirt on hospital rounds over the holidays.

(By the way, we did locate my elderly patient later in the day of my visit. She had wandered half a mile toward town and was found at the Safeway store walking the aisles.)

# Measles

I remember suffering with measles as a third grader. My eyes hurt severely. My brothers and I stayed in a darkened room, because light only increased the eye pain. My mother had difficulty controlling the high fevers. I remember aching so badly that I could barely walk. My coughing was harsh and persistent to the point that I couldn't speak. Sometimes, I coughed hard enough to have trouble breathing.

After we were miserable for several days, Doctor P.E. Wally came to our home to examine us. He prescribed some awful tasting tea that my mom forced us to drink to bring out the rash. I do not know whether it was the tea working or the natural progression of the disease, but my fever abated and a rash appeared soon thereafter. I recall the rash causing a profound itching that my mom treated with a terrible smelling cream that was also prescribed by Doctor Wally.

In my sophomore biology class, I learned about the scourges of humanity. My teacher told us that vaccines would be developed someday to eliminate these infections. The polio vaccine had almost eliminated polio within a few years, and now the new measles vaccine promised to do the same for measles.

In medical school, I learned about mumps, measles, rubella, and chickenpox, the "common childhood diseases." Our infectious disease professor, however, cautioned us, "Vaccines have almost eliminated these diseases. You may never see them in practice."

While in medical school, I had the good fortune to see and examine kids with these diseases during a pediatric experience with indigent children.

During my pediatric rotation as an intern, I had the opportunity to care for several children with measles who had slipped through the immunization net because of religious objections by the parents. My pediatric preceptor told me I was lucky to see the kids with measles because the disease was becoming "a rare bird." He thought I might never see another case.

While in private practice in the mid 1980s, I had a college student come into my office one morning during his spring break vacation. This fellow told me he had the flu. He was wearing sunglasses because the light made his eyes hurt. He complained of severe muscle aches, a runny nose, a severe cough that was almost constant, and fevers up to 103 degrees. He wanted some medicine to get well quickly. He didn't want to waste his entire vacation being sick.

I examined this young man in a darkened room because his eyes' sensitivity to light was profound. His eyes were red. His nose was plugged with clear mucous. Once it started, his cough was harsh and unremitting. His lungs were clear, and his heart examination was normal. He had generalized muscle aches. I thought all of these physical findings could be consistent with influenza.

When I looked into the young man's mouth, however, I saw something that I thought I would probably never see again. Next to his back molars on the adjacent soft tissue were white spots with red halos that were known in medicine as Koplik spots. I knew that these spots are seen only with measles. They occur before the rash starts and may be visible for only a short time.

To be sure of my assumption, I performed a test for influenza. When the test was negative, I asked the fellow to return home to bed. I asked him to call me the next day to tell me how he was doing.

He agreed.

The next morning, the college student telephoned me at my office. He told me that he developed a rash sometime during the night. He was now covered with a rash from his head to his thighs. In addition, his fever was less.

I asked him not to leave his home and said I would be right over to look at his rash.

I told my nurse that I was going to make an emergency house call, and I drove the short distance in town to the young man's home.

I met the fellow's mother at the door, and she led me into his bedroom. Dark blankets were strung over the windows to keep out the light to decrease her son's eye pain. My examination revealed a confluent rash that now almost covered the face and chest. Red spots now covered the remainder of his body.

I told the mother that I thought her son had measles.

She replied, "But he had the shots when he was a baby."

I could not give her more of an explanation. However, I asked to perform a test on his blood that would be sent to the state lab for confirmation. (Now, a special test can be done more rapidly on the cells found in the nose secretions.) Until I received the confirmation test report, I thought my patient should remain at home.

The mom agreed.

Her son felt so bad that he offered no resistance to having his blood drawn.

The blood was obtained and sent away to the state lab. I called the state lab to inform them of my suspicions and asked them to expedite the testing.

Within a few days, people from the State Health Department were in my office investigating a case of measles.

Over the next several weeks, I visited twelve children at their homes with measles, just like Doctor P.E. Wally visited me when I was a boy. Their physical findings were just as I remembered them when I was a child with measles. Interestingly, all the kids I evaluated had received measles vaccinations as infants.

Before the nearby schools dismissed that spring, the local health department held a campaign to immunize all children for measles. All kids in the junior high school received a second immunization.

Eventually, it was determined that my college student was infected at his college in Minnesota. The college had a measles outbreak that spring too. The public health authorities traced the source of the infection to a student from Canada who had never received immunizations and became infected with the virus.

With the beginning of the next college year, many colleges required documentation of a measles immunization that was given immediately before entering school. This meant that some students received a third immunization. As far as I know, the additional immunizations did not cause any problems with the recipients.

As time passed, investigators determined that a single shot of the measles vaccine had a five to ten percent failure rate. In addition, after 10 to 15 years, another group of recipients gradually lost their immunity to measles. Therefore, the Public Health Service issued a recommendation that a second measles immunization be given to all children entering junior high school.

Our measles *epidemic* in Sidney included over thirty cases.

Over the next twenty years, I did not see another case of measles.

# Merry Christmas

The winter of 1983 was one of the coldest on record in Sidney, Montana. On Friday, December 23, an official record low temperature of minus forty degrees Fahrenheit was recorded in the early morning hours. The red dye in the mercury thermometer that hung outside our kitchen window was only half way up the bubble and well below the minus forty degree mark. One of my neighbors told me his barn thermometer read a mere minus fifty-two degrees that morning. The official recorded maximum temperature for the day was a balmy minus twenty-five degrees! With the addition of some brisk winds, the wind chill index plunged to near eighty degrees below zero.

The duties of caring for the sick and the injured, however, never stop in a small community. The hospital and the medical clinics were open for business as usual.

At the time, our community was in the midst of several severe communicable disease outbreaks simultaneously. Influenza, para influenza, respiratory syncytial virus (RSV), croup, and common cold infections were playing havoc with the county's inhabitants. It seemed that all the clinics, the nursing home, the pharmacies and the hospital emergency room had been packed with sick people for days on end.

As this day progressed, the weather deteriorated. Brisk winds along with a little snow produced blizzard conditions and icy roads. Driving an automobile became a treacherous adventure even for the most experienced winter weather drivers. In response to the deteriorating weather and road conditions, the patients who were on my clinic schedule that day started to cancel their appointments.

My office staff noted that many of the patients who were canceling their appointments either sounded quite ill on the telephone or they were caring for elderly parents or children who were ill. My nurse informed me that she had told a number of patients to go to the emergency room if they got worse or to call the ambulance.

Since the hospital administration had been reluctant over the years to clear the snow from our combined clinic and hospital parking lots early in the mornings before patients arrived, I had taken the initiative to buy a snowplow for my Dodge pickup. I used the snowplow to clear our parking lot after snowstorms and before I made hospital rounds in the mornings. I also used the plow to get myself through country snowdrifts on my way to and from work. I had driven my pickup with its snowplow attached to work this day.

I decided to send my office staff home early because of the weather. Before leaving, however, I asked my nurse to make a list for me of the people who had cancelled their appointments along with their complaints and their in-town addresses. I asked my staff to call the patients on the list to tell them that I would be making a house call sometime that afternoon or early evening. Before my employees left the clinic, I wished them a safe trip home and a Merry Christmas.

Afterward, I went to the clinic pharmacy and loaded a box with various antibiotics for adults and kids, cough medicines, antiviral medicines, Tylenol and whatever else I thought I would usually prescribe for the infectious illnesses I had been seeing the clinic. Instead of making a bill on the spot, the pharmacist agreed to let me pay for whatever I used when I returned.

I remember the thermometer in my office window read minus twenty-eight degrees. When I walked to my pickup, the wind was brutally cold. The inside of my windshield frosted over almost as soon as my warm body got inside the cab. I started my pickup's engine and then walked back inside my office to wait for the engine to warm enough to defrost the windows. While inside, I remembered to telephone my wife at home to let her know what I was doing and when I anticipated being home.

When my pickup was warm and its windows were defrosted, I headed out to make my house calls. The blizzard made visibility poor and produced substantial drifting on the city's streets. I needed my snowplow to reach about half of the homes in town that were on my list. At each home, I met with some really sick people. I saw elderly patients alone at home who were quite ill with influenza. I treated some parents who were just as ill as their kids. I saw a little girl with a temperature of 104 degrees just after she had suffered a seizure because of her fever. After I held the naked child for about five minutes outside in below zero temperatures, her temperature normalized and her mental status improved. I even treated a next-door neighbor of one of my patients who had come to help his neighbor, and who also had pneumonia. At each home, I met folks who were thankful for my efforts.

Most people questioned me why I was making house calls in such bad weather before the holidays.

I told them that since I had a pickup truck equipped with a snowplow, it seemed easier for me to get to them than for them to get to me.

When a patient would offer me a payment for my efforts and the medicines, I refused. I just wished them a Merry Christmas!

I must have made twelve home visits during my trek and treated more than twenty patients.

Driving three miles through the blizzard to get home was another adventure.

# Bugged

One day in the late fall, the charge nurse and I had been treating patients in our emergency room all night. About 4 a.m. we heard people yelling to get in at the front door of the emergency room. As the nurse and I walked into the atrium of the hospital, we saw three men. Each man was dressed in hunting fatigues. Two of the men were pounding on the locked glass door because the security latch was engaged. The men were yelling at the same time, so I could not discern what their issue was. However, it appeared to me that one fellow was much more agitated than his friends.

After the nurse allowed them into the hospital, two of the men continued to talk loudly and rapidly as they tried to explain their situation. The third man, on the other hand, was acting quite strangely. While babbling about aliens invading his brain, the man pounded on the left side of his head with ferocious blows. He even started to hit his head against a wall.

Since the problem appeared to be with the third hunter, the nurse had the larger of the other two companions assist her with maneuvering the agitated man into the emergency room for an examination. Meanwhile, I took the third man aside to get some information about his agitated companion.

The man, who still smelled of alcohol, told me that their hunting party, which included four hunters three days before, had been on a week-long elk and deer hunting trip many miles from town out in the boondocks. The fourth hunter owned a hunting shack in the area. The group had good luck and used all their wild game tags the first two days of their hunt. Since the fourth man knew the roads in the area best, he left the trio on the third day to replenish their booze supply. The remaining trio decided to play card games and drink booze until their friend returned.

The man told me that, unfortunately, the weather turned sour. A blizzard came in overnight, and no travel was allowed. Their friend was stranded in a nearby town in a motel while the trio was stuck in the hunting cabin with no place to go. Since they had plentiful food, and more than enough beer and whiskey, the hunters were not concerned. They planned to ride out the storm and wait for their buddy. The remaining hunters started playing cards and drinking booze.

Reportedly, the card games and the drinking continued well into the night and the men became quite drunk in the process. Two of the men fell asleep on their cots. The third man fell asleep at the kitchen table with the light still on. Sometime during the early morning darkness, with the blizzard roaring outside, the hunter at the table started screaming about his head being invaded by aliens. The man started to pound on his head and his ears with his hands. When he tried to stand up, the hunter ran into walls or fell down. The remaining two men were at a loss as what they could do. They had no telephone to summon help, and, if they did get help, nobody could get to them because of the weather. The shack had no telephone. (This was before everyone had cell phones.)

The man related that the two friends tried to console their hunting buddy any way they could. However, the man acted like a raving maniac for more than thirty hours before he collapsed from exhaustion. The two men wondered if their friend just couldn't hold his liquor and would be okay when he woke up. When a sheriff rescue team arrived in the night about forty hours later, the man awoke only to start acting crazy again. The rescue team transported all the hunters to their parked vehicles. Subsequently, the two men transported their friend to the nearest medical facility, which was our hospital.

After hearing this intriguing tale, I walked into the emergency room to see my patient. He was pacing around the room waving his arms shouting, "It's in my ear. It's driving me crazy!" At that point, the man started to slap at his left ear with his hand quite vigorously.

I asked the man to sit on the examination table so I could examine him.

He exclaimed, "I can't. It won't let me!"

I asked the man if he could stand still long enough for me to look into his ear with a flashlight.

He replied, "I'll try, but hurry up."

From my medical bag I retrieved my otoscope (a fancy name for a small flashlight) to look into ears. With just a passing glance I could see that a winged critter had flown into the man's ear canal and was flapping its wings in an attempt to escape. I told the patient he had a bug in his ear.

He yelled out, "Well, kill the damn thing!"

I wondered how I could best kill this insect. I knew the emergency room would have something readily available I could use. I asked the nurse to find some mineral oil or something like it.

Within moments, the charge nurse found a bottle of viscous lidocaine, a topical anesthetic medication. The nurse had a good idea because this stuff will not only suffocate the bug but would also numb the ear canal.

My patient asserted, "Well, what the hell are you waiting on? Quit jawing and kill it!"

I asked the man to tip his head sideways so I could put the medicine into his ear. After I inserted a few drops of a topical anesthetic medication into his ear canal, the man asked me if he could lie down. His agitation ceased almost immediately. His head clapping stopped. The man literally collapsed from exhaustion.

A few minutes later, while my patient was lying down, I took a pair of tweezers and extracted a large dead moth from the man's left ear canal. The nurse put the critter into a specimen bottle as a souvenir.

The hunter rested for a short time before he and his hunting buddies started to leave the ER. I told them to go home and get a good rest.

One of the men replied, "We gotta go back now. We left our guns and our animals at the hunting shack."

# False Hopes

I was making hospital rounds one morning in the mid 1990s when I received a page from the emergency room nurse. The nurse told me that she had a patient named Elmer Harrison in the emergency room who was requesting a lung CAT scan (CAT stands for computerized axial tomography, a special kind of x-ray procedure). When I asked her why the patient needed a CAT scan, she said, "All I know is that Doctor Barrigan (our local surgeon) was asked first, and he told me to call you."

Somewhat intrigued, I called Doctor Barrigan who told me that this fellow had some kind of lung issue. The man's doctor in Billings wanted a CAT scan with a report pronto. Since the man's issue was medical, and not surgical, Doctor Barrigan passed the patient on to me.

I thought to myself, "What the heck. If the doc wants the scan, his patient can have the scan." I asked the nurse to arrange for the patient to have the CAT scan performed when possible. I then went back to making my hospital rounds.

An hour or so later, I received a call from the hospital's radiologist who said, "Hey, Jim, I've got this chest CAT scan on a man named Harrison that looks pretty ugly. What's the story?"

I told the radiologist what I knew about the man, which was essentially nothing. I told the radiologist that a doctor in Billings wanted the test, so I ordered it.

The radiologist asked me to come to his office and review the pictures. He wanted me to evaluate the guy too because he was having trouble breathing.

After this conversation, I went directly to the radiologist's reading room where he showed me the CAT scan of the man that revealed both lungs full of tumor. A plain x-ray of the chest revealed additional anomalies in the lungs.

When I went to see Mr. Harrison in the x-ray room, I found him to be short of breath but able to talk if he took his time. The man's blood oxygen level was low enough to indicate to me that he had a serious pulmonary problem.

I advised Mr. Harrison that his CAT scan showed something going on in his lungs.

He told me that he knew that. He had doctors in Billings and in Miles City who had been treating him for it.

I asked the fellow if he knew what disease he had in his lungs, but he did not.

After this, I told Mr. Harrison that I thought I should admit him to the hospital so I could sort things out a bit and so he could get some lung treatment to improve his breathing.

He agreed.

I made a telephone call to the doctor in Billings, but he was out of town. I telephoned the doctor in Miles City who practiced at the local radiation cancer facility and talked to his receptionist. The woman told me that the radiation oncologist was busy, but he agreed to call me back soon.

About half an hour later I received the call from the Miles City physician. I asked him about our mutual patient's disease. He said, "Oh yeah. He's been seeing a doc in Billings for some time. We've been trying to reduce the size of his lung tumor with radiation."

When I inquired about the kind of tumor the patient had, the oncologist told me, "He's got a mesothelioma."[26] Then he said, "If he's having some trouble you can send him down here for another treatment."

With this information in hand I went to the library to learn as much as I could in a short time about mesothelioma. Also, I talked briefly with our hospital's pathologist. In the 1990s the average survival for a patient with mesothelioma was less than a year after the diagnosis was made. The five-year survival rate was zero! Mr. Harrison's doctors knew this and yet continued to treat him instead of telling him the truth about his disease. (In 2010, the average survival time was no better, but the five-year survival rate had improved slightly to less than five percent.)

Armed with a lot more information about Mr. Harrison, his disease, and the care he had already received, I went to take his history. Mr. Harrison told me that he had been ill for almost five years. During the interview Mr. Harrison said his doctors had told him that after five years of treatment he would be cured.

---

[26] Mesothelioma is an uncommon type of lung cancer that has about an 80 percent correlation with asbestos exposure. The tumor may arise up to 40 years after an asbestos exposure. About 2000 cases are reported annually in the United States. Smoking related cases of lung cancer account for about 180,000 new cases per year.

I thought to myself, "This is not possible. Why would somebody tell a patient with a disease carrying a five-year survival rate of zero that he would be cured after five years of treatment?"

I took it upon myself to relate to Mr. Harrison what I had learned about his problem from his doctors and what I knew from the literature. I informed Mr. Harrison that his doctors knew how bad his disease was and, unfortunately, their communications to him must have been misunderstood.

Mr. Harrison said he did not misunderstand the doctors; I could ask his wife because she was there too.

I told Mr. Harrison that, with what I knew from the literature, his life expectancy was very short. After I presented him with the survival data, I told him that mesothelioma had no cure. I asked him if he had a will or had he talked with anyone about a will. If not, I suggested that he consider doing so.

Mr. Harrison became incensed with me. He shouted, "You're a lying son-of-a-bitch and a quack! I'm getting out of here!"

Mr. Harrison and his wife stormed out of our hospital.

I learned later that he returned that day to Miles City where he received more radiation treatments. Soon after leaving our hospital Mr. Harrison suffered a pulmonary arrest at another hospital and was placed on a mechanical ventilator to breathe. Subsequently, he was transferred by airplane to the Mayo Clinic in Rochester, Minnesota, where he was kept alive on the ventilator in their intensive care unit. The doctors at Mayo knew Mr. Harrison's death was imminent and wanted to stop the ventilator. However, the family did not want Mr. Harrison to die in Minnesota. Therefore, the Mayo doctors kept Mr. Harrison on the mechanical ventilator and transported him back to Montana by airplane. He died soon after returning to Montana.

I learned later that Mrs. Harrison considered me responsible for her husband's death.

# Heinz 57

Sidney, Montana, has a restaurant on the south edge of town called the Triangle Night Club. During the oil boom of the 1970s and early 1980s, the Triangle was the place to enjoy good food, drinks, and dancing. The business was packed on the weekends with local residents and oilfield workers having a good time.

One Saturday evening in mid 1970s, I was on duty in the emergency room when the hospital received a call from the local Law Enforcement Center. The dispatcher requested that an ambulance be sent to the Triangle Night Club. (This was our system of emergency communication for our county before a 911 exchange was installed in the 1980s.) The dispatcher told the emergency room nurse that there had been a fight in the restaurant, and that one person was in serious condition with a knife wound. The dispatcher informed us that the nightclub was packed with patrons and that law enforcement officers were on the scene for crowd control. The emergency room nurse radio-paged the volunteer ambulance personnel on call. Within a few minutes, the ambulance with two EMTs aboard raced the three miles to the Triangle.

A short time later, one of the EMTs reported to the emergency room nurse that they had a middle-aged female victim lying on the dance floor with a knife sticking out of her chest. The victim was coherent. Her vital signs were normal. The EMT noted that they would transport the woman when they had stabilized the knife in the chest. Their ETA (estimated time of arrival) was fifteen minutes.

When I asked about other victims in the fight, the EMT told me there was no fight. He reported that the sheriff had a guy in custody and only our patient had an injury.

After the ambulance had arrived back at the hospital and the EMTs had transported their patient to the emergency room examination cart, I asked one of the EMTs if he had any additional history for me.

All the EMT knew was that some guy stabbed this woman while they were dancing.

Our patient was alert and coherent. She was not distressed. Her vital signs were good. She displayed no signs of breathing difficulty. The EMTs had secured the knife with enough duct tape that it would never move. This situation hampered my examination, but my brief examination of the woman's chest was unremarkable. (The knife was not removed because one never knows what may be damaged. Secured in place the knife could do no further damage.)

I had a chest x-ray performed that revealed that the knife had not penetrated the woman's chest cavity. A rib had deflected the knife, and the knife blade settled just underneath the skin. I showed the x-ray to my patient.

Now that I knew my patient was stable and would not require surgery, I removed the duct tape holding the knife in place. On the woman's chest wall and around the entry wound was a reddish-brown substance. When I commented about the substance, the woman told us the reddish stuff was steak sauce.

I asked the woman if she could tell the nurse and me what happened.

Now that the woman knew she was not seriously injured, she became mad, really mad. She told us that the man who tried to kill her was her husband. The woman explained that they were celebrating their wedding anniversary at the Triangle that evening. After eating their steak dinners, the husband asked my patient to dance. When they started dancing, the husband kissed his wife, whispered, "I love you," in her ear, and then stabbed her with his dirty steak knife. The woman told us that, before this episode, their years together had been wonderful.

Within months, the pair was divorced.

As far as I know, the husband was charged with attempted murder, convicted, and sent to prison.

# What Price For Glory?

I was working in the emergency room on a weekend in early November. I had spent most of the weekend tending to the injuries incurred by some of the locals as they enjoyed their favorite outdoors activities such as riding horses, riding motorcycles, hunting, and adventuring the county's back roads on all-terrain vehicles. By early evening on Sunday the influx of trauma patients had subsided, and I was ready to go home.

As I was completing the charting for my last emergency room patient, the nurse called out to tell me that another patient was coming in from the parking lot.

Within a few minutes, the nurse accompanied by the young man's parents brought a teenage male into the emergency room. The nurse told me, "The parents said he collapsed at home."

Upon further inquiry, the parents told me that they had been at a wrestling meet on Saturday in Great Falls, Montana, a city about four hundred miles from Sidney. The family spent Saturday night in Great Falls and then made the eight-hour drive to Sidney on Sunday. Their son had won his wrestling match and the mother noted that he seemed to be just fine afterward.

Additionally, the father, whose breath smelled of alcohol, told me that his son had no complaints that morning except for the usual aches and pains after wrestling. The father said with pride that he had a pretty tough kid.

The parents noted that their son didn't eat much on the way home. However, since the wrestlers were always fasting to maintain their weights, neither parent thought anything was out of the ordinary.

The nurse reported that the boy's blood pressure was low and his pulse was high. I knew this finding was consistent with my patient being short of intravascular volume, either from dehydration or from loss of blood.

Finally, I had a chance to talk with the patient. He told me that he was thrown down hard during his match and landed on his left side. In addition, the boy informed me that he had sore ribs on the left side after the match but thought he was just bruised.

When I asked the teenager why he didn't eat during the trip home, he said he had a stomachache and felt like throwing up.

My young patient appeared uncomfortable lying on the examination bed. My examination revealed point tenderness in the left upper quadrant of his abdomen with reflex guarding of the abdominal muscles to even gentle pressure. I suspected that the young man had an injured spleen. I also suspected that he had blood in his abdomen.

I repeated the boy's pulse and blood pressure lying down and standing. Lying down, the blood pressure was low, and the pulse was normal. (Just what I would expect from a well-conditioned athlete.) Upon standing, however, the boy's blood pressure dropped to a point where I could not feel his pulse. The young man became faint and I promptly laid him back down upon the examination bed.

I told the nurse that our patient needed some fluids *now*! While I started a large intravenous catheter, the nurse located the needed intravenous fluids. After I was successful in inserting the intravenous catheter, I withdrew some blood for analysis. After the nurse attached the IV fluid bag, I asked her to run the fluid in at a maximum rate and then notify the laboratory technician.

Our hospital had recently installed a CAT scanner. This diagnostic x-ray is good for evaluating the solid organs for damage such as the spleen, liver, and kidneys, and to look for abnormal accumulations of blood. Fortunately, the x-ray technician on-call for emergencies lived only a short distance from the hospital.

While the x-ray technician was coming to the hospital, I called Doctor Barrigan, our local general surgeon, to apprise him of my situation. I told him that he might have to do a splenectomy before supper. Doctor Barrigan agreed to meet my patient and me in the CAT scan room ASAP (a soon as possible). The emergency room nurse and I transported our patient to radiology for his CAT scan.

By the time we arrived in the radiology department and transferred our patient onto the CAT scanner table, which was just another few minutes, our 1000-milliliter IV bag was nearly empty. I repeated my patient's vital signs. His blood pressure and pulse were unchanged but no worse. I was encouraged. The nurse hung another bag of fluid to run in at the maximum rate.

Doctor Barrigan arrived before the radiology technician had performed the CAT scan. After examining the teenager, he agreed with my assessment.

When the CAT scan was completed, Doctor Barrigan and I made unofficial readings of the films. We agreed that the scan revealed a tear in the capsule of the spleen and some free blood in the abdomen.

In years past the treatment for an injured spleen was an immediate surgical removal. However, since the mid-1970s, spleen injuries in children were treated with cautious and careful observation. Often the bleeding from the spleen would stop by itself, and the spleen would heal nicely if given enough time.

After discussing our patient's status, our mutual decision was to replace the boy's vascular volume and to observe him carefully in the hospital. Before leaving for home, Doctor Barrigan said he would ask the nurses to call him with updates during the night.

As the nurse and radiology technician transferred our patient back to the emergency room to await the preparation of his hospital bed, I talked with the parents about their son. I informed them that he had a ruptured spleen, but we hoped that he would not require emergency surgery that night. I outlined the therapy plan that Doctor Barrigan and I had agreed upon. I also told the parents that their son's wrestling season was over.

When I mentioned the end of their son's wrestling season, the intoxicated father slurred something like, "What do you mean he can't wrestle? He's going to be the State champion!"

I repeated to the parents that their son would not be cleared to wrestle for at least eight to twelve weeks even if he did not have surgery.

The father shouted back, "What do you mean he can't wrestle?"

I repeated that his son's injury would take months to heal and that I would not clear him to wrestle for the remainder of the season.

Pointing his finger at me, the father said, "Why don't we take a walk outside and settle this little misunderstanding man to man?"

Bewildered that this man would endanger his son's life so he could have the satisfaction of watching him wrestle, I just looked at him. I was speechless.

The son came to my rescue. He told his dad to go home.

When his father gave his son an angry stare, he repeated, "Dad, just go home."

The mother chimed in and told her husband that it was time for them to go home.

Doctor Barrigan and I observed the teenager for a few days in the hospital. Fortunately, his bleeding stopped and his vital signs and blood test results stabilized.

While my patient was hospitalized, I had a discussion with the wrestling coach who promptly removed him from that year's wrestling squad.

Over the next few months the young man recovered. He was ready for wrestling camps in the summer. He wrestled on the varsity squad for several more years. Unfortunately, the young man was never the State champion wrestler his father wanted, but he enjoyed a successful high school wrestling career.

# Making a Difference

Give to the world the best you have and
the best will come back to you.

Author unknown c.1780

# Beatrice

I first met sixty-six-year-old Beatrice in the emergency department. The ambulance crew brought her to the hospital after she had collapsed at her home while babysitting. She complained of discomfort going down both her arms and severe pressure between her breasts. She told me that she had similar discomforts the night before but did not want to bother anyone since it was late. Besides, after an hour or so, the feelings got better. She told me that she had been a perfectly healthy person with no problems.

Beatrice was an awful historian. She had been in the hospital once years before, but she could not remember why. She was a widow but did not recall when or why her husband died. She had three children and a few family members who lived nearby. Throughout my history taking, Beatrice kept saying that she didn't want to be a bother.

An electrocardiogram (ECG) (heart tracing) was done in the emergency department that showed evidence for an acute myocardial infarction (heart attack).

When I was assured that my patient was as stable as possible, I arranged for her to be transferred to our Intensive Care Unit. Within minutes of her ICU arrival, Beatrice went into shock. Her blood pressure dropped to almost nothing. Her pulse became erratic and then quite slow with a heart rate down to about thirty beats per minute. Her ECG revealed a sequence of multiple rhythm abnormalities that finally ended with a complete heart block pattern (This is not unusual with acute heart attacks. The usual reason for death with heart attacks is a rhythm disorder with shock).

Promptly our ICU team instituted advanced cardiac life support treatment protocols (ACLS) for shock with complete heart block. After giving Beatrice a variety of heart medications over about thirty minutes, her heart rhythm and blood pressure stabilized. However, her ECG continued to show evidence of an irritable heart and electrical conduction problems.

Beatrice's condition remained marginal through the night. The following morning her heart rhythm changed into a complete heart block pattern again. I knew the only way to prevent her

death was to insert a pacemaker. Therefore, I asked Doctor
Berryman, our local internist, to evaluate Beatrice and to insert
a temporary pacemaker. Doctor Berryman successfully inserted
the pacemaker, and Beatrice's cardiovascular system had immediate improvement.

Despite a complicated stay in the ICU, the temporary pacemaker was removed after about a week. Although the damage to
her heart had been significant, Beatrice was able to go home
from the hospital after about two weeks.

Doctor Berryman noted that her chances for living five years
were not good.

Beatrice came to my office about six months later. Again, in
her mild-mannered quiet way, Beatrice apologized for bothering
me with her problems, but she said she just didn't feel good. Her
blood pressure had escalated to 170/110 (170 over 110; 120/80 is
normal). Just a few weeks before, it had been 120/70. When she
left the hospital after her heart attack, the blood pressure was
about 100/70. I just knew something was amiss. After extensive
testing, Doctor Berryman and I could find only that Beatrice had
developed severe high blood pressure for an unknown reason.
(High blood pressure forces the heart to work harder; Beatrice's
damaged heart did not need an extra workload.)

After another week in the hospital, we were able to control
Beatrice's hypertension with a combination of medications.
Again, she was allowed to go home to recuperate.

Over the next year or so, I had Beatrice come to the office to be
evaluated. Each time her blood pressure was elevated and each
time she would tell me something like, "I hate to bother you, but
I don't feel very good today." Each visit I would make a medication adjustment to bring her pressure under control.

One day after Beatrice had gone home from my office, I finally
realized that she may just have white coat hypertension, a phenomenon whereby a patient's blood pressure goes up substantially just because of the stress of going to, visiting, or even
thinking about a doctor. I telephoned Beatrice and asked if I
could come to her home after work that day to take her blood
pressure.

She agreed and instructed me how to get to her home.

Beatrice lived in a quiet part of town on a street with minimal
traffic. She had a quaint mobile home with a well-maintained
yard and many flowers. When I knocked on the door she said in
her quiet voice, "Come on in. The door's always open."

I found Beatrice resting in her La-Z-Boy chair. She told me she was tired.

After a bit of small talk, I asked Beatrice if I could examine her in her chair. She responded with, "Oh my, of course."

I asked her how she felt, and she told me that she was just fine.

My examination was unremarkable just like it had been a few hours earlier in my office. However, Beatrice's blood pressure, which had been 180/110 in my office a few hours before, was now a normal 120/80. When I asked Beatrice to stand up, she said she didn't feel good again. When I took her blood pressure standing, it dropped to 80/60. I knew that Beatrice felt poorly not because her blood pressure was too high, but because I had overmedicated her and it was too low.

After Beatrice sat down, she started to feel better. I told her that I did not want her to come to my office anymore.

Before I could finish my sentence, Beatrice became teary-eyed and wanted to know what she had done wrong.

I reassured Beatrice that she had done nothing wrong. I told her that her blood pressure went way too high when she came into my office. Therefore, I wanted permission to come to her house to see her instead. I told her that I did not want to put any more stress on her heart than necessary.

After thinking for a few moments, Beatrice told me that my coming to her home would be such a bother for me.

I reassured her that I passed near her home often. Besides, it was only a short walk from my office, and I could always use the exercise.

She relented by saying, "Well, I guess that will be all right."

From that day forward, I took Beatrice's blood pressure daily at her home, including weekends. Over the next month and after I had changed her medication dosages, her blood pressures stabilized. I visited her once a week for almost a year. Her blood pressures remained good. Thereafter, I arranged for a county nurse to visit Beatrice weekly and send her reports to me. I continued to visit Beatrice on a monthly basis for the next twelve years.

Fourteen years after her first heart attack, Beatrice sustained another small heart attack and was admitted to the hospital. Again she apologized for being such a nuisance. This episode left her already enlarged heart with a rhythm problem called atrial fibrillation[27] during which the upper heart chambers beat irregularly and out of rhythm with the lower heart chambers. She required more medications to anti-coagulate her blood and to keep her heart from beating too fast. My patient, however, was able to return home. The county nurses and I resumed our home visits.

About a year later, Beatrice came to my office because she couldn't catch her breath. After a brief examination, I sent her straight to the hospital. She had suffered another small heart attack that made her mild heart failure become severe heart failure. Even though she could barely breathe, Beatrice quietly let me know that she was sorry to be such a bother.

Again I was able to arrange for Beatrice to go home by coordinating a team consisting of family members, neighbors, county nurses, and me to watch her.

Beatrice seemed to manage at home with the aid of her angels, a name she used collectively for her care team members. Another four years elapsed before her next significant event. (This was now eighteen years after her first heart attack and after we thought her chances of living for five years were small.)

Beatrice's granddaughter brought her to the emergency room complaining of severe abdominal pain on the right side. The local general surgeon who examined her initially noted astutely that she did not have a surgical problem. He thought her pain might be due to liver engorgement from acute heart failure. It was.

Again, Beatrice spent some time in the hospital to remove excess fluid from her lungs. I noticed on this admission that Beatrice's mental function had decreased substantially from my last visit with her. She had developed significant confusion and memory difficulties. Knowing that she still had atrial fibrillation, I presumed that she had incurred a small stroke or multiple strokes (again, a common occurrence with atrial fibrillation).

I did not think my patient should go home after this hospitalization. However, after some vigorous persuasion by Beatrice and her family, I relented and allowed Beatrice to return to her home once again. She had minimal resources to pay for any care

---

[27] Atrial fibrillation is a common heart rhythm disorder in the aging or damaged heart characterized by chaotic electrical activity in the atria or upper chambers of the heart. This chaotic activity produces an irregular heartbeat. Common complications of atrial fibrillation include strokes and blood pressure instability.

outside of Medicare, and she he did not qualify for Medicaid (a common dilemma with the elderly). I made sure that arrangements were made with even more people to care for Beatrice at her home.

The care team struggled for about a year to keep Beatrice at home. However, her dementia worsened. The granddaughter related numerous episodes of confusion, forgetfulness, and bizarre behavior. The members of the care team, which included Home Health, County Health, close family, church members, neighbors, and friends, had finally decided that caring for Beatrice at her home had now become too difficult.

After a mandatory three-day stay in the hospital for her heart failure (a Medicare rule to authorize Medicare payments to the nursing home), Beatrice was admitted to the local nursing home.

At the age of eighty-five and soon before her death (now more than nineteen years after her first heart attack), I was asked to see Beatrice at the nursing home. I found her sleeping soundly in a chair, and I was able to examine her without disturbing her sleep. On her lap I saw a letter that she was composing. It said, "Dear Dr. Ashcraft, I know I have been a bother all these years, but you are my guardian angel. I love you."

Beatrice died a few days later.

Beatrice was one of those kind, wonderful souls who nobody ever forgets.

# Florence

At the age of fourteen, Florence was infected with polio. She was totally paralyzed below the chest for nine months. Thereafter, she regained the ability to walk slowly. However, she never improved enough to run, skip, or hop with the other kids. Later in life when she started to date, Florence learned to slow dance.

As a child, Florence was often ill with respiratory illnesses. Her mother had suffered with allergies and asthma for years, but nobody considered that Florence could have asthma too. Florence was finally diagnosed with having asthma when she was in her late teens. She was a rebellious girl and did not want to appear ill or weak. Therefore, she seldom took her asthma medications as her doctors had recommended.

Florence's mother smoked cigarettes despite having constant breathing problems. Like her mother, Florence became a smoker as a teenager.

Florence married when she was in her early twenties and soon had a child. Caring for her child was difficult because her polio-weakened muscles fatigued easily, but she managed with frequent periods of rest. After her child entered school, Florence worked as a sales clerk to help provide for her family. As the years passed, she became increasingly unable to perform jobs requiring physical activity because her polio-scarred muscles gradually worsened.

Florence relieved her muscular pain and family stress by smoking heavily and drinking alcohol. Eventually, she was smoking more than three packages of cigarettes per day and often would drink herself to sleep. Despite frequent episodes of asthma or lung infections, Florence continued to smoke cigarettes.

Through the years, many doctors treated Florence for her asthma. However, to save the family's precious few dollars, she used her medications sporadically. She tried to get by with over-the-counter asthma drugs when she was short of money, but these medications didn't work very well. One doctor even gave her antibiotics to take two weeks out of every month in an attempt to keep her from having episodes of pneumonia or bronchitis. All the doctors encouraged Florence to stop smoking to no avail.

I met Florence for the first time on an emergency basis when she was fifty-five years old. Whispering, Florence told me that she was having more trouble breathing than usual and had been ill for months. Florence advised me that she smoked too much and had emphysema. She had tried to stop smoking but just couldn't.

My first impression of Florence was that she was going to die in my office. I had a fifty-five-year-old woman who looked eighty and was gray. I could hear no air movement in her lungs. Fortunately, after performing a few maneuvers in the office with medications, my patient's lungs opened up, and she could talk better. Her color, however, remained gray. I had my nurse call ahead to the hospital to get a bed ready. I then placed Florence in a wheelchair and pushed her to the intensive care unit.

In the ICU after her condition had improved, Florence told me that she had not been able to work for several weeks. Because of her weak muscles, she could barely walk. She had been sleeping sitting upright for as long as she could remember. Her only breathing medicine was a Bronkaid Mist, an over-the-counter product that was not working. Additionally, Florence told me she had something wrong with her heart, had high blood pressure, and couldn't afford medicines.

After consulting with an internal medicine specialist, who thought Florence also had heart failure to complicate her emphysema, asthma, pneumonia, and post-polio weakness, our team gave Florence as much as our hospital could offer in pulmonary care. When she had improved only slightly after twenty-four hours of intensive pulmonary care, we decided to transport Florence to Billings for more intensive pulmonary care. After a week or more in Billings, Florence returned home improved but not well.

Because of her increasing difficulty walking and breathing, I visited Florence at her home. (I figured it was easier for me to go a few blocks out of my way in a car than to have my sick patient struggle for several hours to make a clinic visit.) Over the next few months, I was amazed at how her stamina and breathing improved.

Unfortunately, about six months later, Florence's husband could no longer take the stress and left town with a woman twenty years his junior. Florence, in an acutely agitated state, decided to die by drinking booze and taking a handful of pills. She was surprised to awaken in our ICU. Again, after several days of vigorous pulmonary care, Florence left our hospital improved but not well.

With the help of mental health workers, home health assistants, and friends, she barely managed. I evaluated Florence at her home periodically, and her conditions worsened with time as I expected. Despite our best efforts, Florence continued to smoke up to three packages of cigarettes daily. Occasionally, she required hospital care to improve her marginal lung function.

Seven years after I first met Florence in my office, she called me to make a home visit. I left for her home immediately. When I saw Florence sitting in her chair gasping for air, I picked her up and carried her to my pickup. On the way to the hospital, Florence reminded me that she had a living will and she *was not* going to the ICU again!

She struggled to breathe during the night despite our best efforts. The following morning she insisted that I give her a cigarette.

The nurse and I told her that our hospital had a strict no smoking policy in effect. These rules prevented her from smoking in the hospital.

Upon hearing this, Florence became acutely agitated, sat up, and demanded a cigarette.

The nurses and I could see that her agitation was making her breathing worse. I told the nurse, "Get her a cigarette. I will take the blame."

A nurse retrieved a cigarette from Florence's purse, placed it between her lips, and lit it with a lighter that was found in the purse.

Florence thanked us, puffed on the cigarette several times, and abruptly stopped breathing. As the nurse extinguished the cigarette, Florence's heart stopped.

One of the nurses said, "She doesn't have to suffer any more."

Florence was sixty-two years old.

# Madeline

On Thanksgiving Day, recently widowed Madeline Wrightson decided it was time to visit some longtime friends and relatives who lived in the northeastern part of Montana. Since she was now about eighty years old, it just seemed to be the right time to travel before something happened to her. She had postponed this long trip literally for decades. So the Saturday morning after Thanksgiving Day Madeline boarded an eastbound Amtrak train in Spokane, Washington, and headed toward the Sidney, Montana, area to visit her longtime friends.

It was dark when the Amtrak train arrived in Williston, North Dakota. Madeline noticed that she felt odd and relayed that to her friends. They offered to take her to the local hospital, but Madeline assured them that she was just an old woman suffering from a long day of travel and train food. She knew that she was going to be fine. The group then journeyed to the friend's home near Sidney. By the time they arrived, Madeline said she felt fine.

The following morning went well. The old friends became busy outlining events and things to see and do during Madeline's stay.

Shortly after eating lunch, Madeline complained of chest discomfort before losing consciousness. The family members promptly put her in their car and sped the mile or so to the emergency room. At some point during this event, one family member started to perform CPR (cardiopulmonary resuscitation) on Madeline while she was sitting up in the automobile.

Upon their arrival in our hospital parking lot, a nurse noted that Madeline had no pulse or spontaneous respirations. The nurse started CPR in the parking lot and called a CODE.[28] Madeline was transferred to the emergency room where her condition remained unchanged.

The anesthetist and the local general surgeon were in the hospital at the time and responded to the CODE alert. The

---

[28] A CODE is the universal term for a medical emergency in the hospital. Often the term is followed by a color, such as CODE BLUE for a cardiac arrest, or CODE RED for a fire.

emergency team followed ACLS (Advanced Cardiac Life Support) protocols to the letter. Madeline received DC current counter-shocks three times with no improvement in her cardiac status. The anesthetist placed a tube in her trachea (windpipe) so Madeline could be ventilated. When the electrical shocks were not successful, Madeline received adrenalin through her endotracheal tube.

Upon my arrival, the surgeon stood back and allowed me to assume medical control of the CODE.

After the adrenalin had a chance to work, Madeline's heart developed ventricular fibrillation, a rhythm that is not compatible with life. I administered three more DC counter-shocks at 400 watt-seconds, I gave her a bolus of lidocaine (a drug to abort rhythm disturbances), and the nurse started a continuous infusion of lidocaine through an intravenous catheter that had been inserted. The heart monitor now revealed an atrial fibrillation rhythm with a conduction abnormality called a left bundle branch block. Fortunately, Madeline developed a blood pressure. It was low, but it remained stable.

Unfortunately, as her cardiac situation improved, Madeline still did not make any spontaneous breathing efforts, and she remained unresponsive. My concern was that she had suffered a stroke and that we had not done this woman any favors by our resuscitation efforts. Madeline was transferred to our intensive care unit where she was placed on a mechanical ventilator.

When Madeline was settled in the ICU, I inquired about her past medical history. All I discovered was that she was a widow, she had a history of high blood pressure, and her medications were Lasix (a diuretic) and digitalis (a drug to make the heart beat stronger).

Madeline's chest radiograph revealed evidence for heart enlargement and heart failure, not a surprising picture after a cardiac arrest.

My patient's lab data revealed a low potassium level in the blood of only 2.0 (normal is 3.8-5). A low potassium concentration in the blood coupled with digitalis is well known for producing heart arrhythmias. There were no other lab abnormalities, including no evidence for an acute heart attack. The potassium level was corrected promptly with intravenous potassium supplements.

Excluding the fact that she was on a mechanical ventilator, my physical examination of Madeline was unremarkable for her age, except that she was in a coma and showed only a minimal responsiveness to deep pain.

I met with the family and friends outside the ICU. I gave them as much information as I had about Madeline's event and her current condition. I told them that, at that moment, I thought her chances of survival were at best 50:50.

Early the next day my patient still required the ventilator to breathe. Overnight she had developed some curious eye blinking and eye movement activity that suggested seizure activity to me. Later that morning, she developed a grand mal seizure followed by neurological and physical signs that suggested a brainstem injury. Our hospital did not have a CAT scanner at the time to help us decipher Madeline's neurological findings.

I obtained a consultation with our local internist, and together we talked with her family and friends about what our course of action would be if Madeline did indeed have a serious brain injury. Additionally, I called my patient's immediate family and physician in Spokane.

Late the second evening, Madeline started to awaken. Her seizure activity abated. She started to move her arms and legs slowly to commands. She responded to my verbal commands, albeit quite slowly.

Madeline improved exceedingly well over the next several days. Her mental status improved daily, but she had amnesia around the time of her collapse and subsequent treatment. As expected for a woman in her eighties, Madeline became very weak physically. I called in all the rehabilitation folks: physical therapy, speech therapy, and occupational therapy.

After four days on the ventilator, Madeline was weaned from the machine. Unfortunately, she just was not strong enough to breathe for herself long enough and deep enough. Therefore, I placed her back onto the ventilator to wait until she was stronger.

After three or four more days of rest, I was able to slowly wean Madeline off the ventilator. During the entire week or so after the difficult first thirty-six hours, Madeline's blood pressure remained stable, her mental status improved, and her atrial fibrillation rhythm remained unchanged.

Madeline left the Intensive Care Unit on her tenth hospital day.

After multiple discussions with the family members, a decision was made to watch Madeline for several more days until they could arrange for care at their home. Since Madeline planned to stay in Sidney for another week or so before she flew back to Spokane, I kept her physician in Spokane updated on her condition and her plans for aftercare.

Before she left our hospital, a CAT scan of Madeline's head revealed no obvious masses or areas suggesting stroke. Her electrocardiogram reverted to a normal sinus rhythm pattern, but the electrical conduction delay persisted. I never ascertained if that problem was new or old.

Madeline remained in our hospital for a few more days, and then she continued her amazing recovery at her family's home near Sidney.

Madeline made it home to Spokane, Washington, for Christmas. She sent the hospital staff, my office staff, and me holiday cards.

I received a telephone call from Madeline's physician in Spokane about a month later. He told me she was reasonably fit for being eighty years old. He surmised that she had suffered a low blood pressure episode with shock produced by an abnormal heart rhythm. He assumed that the heart arrhythmia was caused by a combination of a low potassium and digitalis. He stopped the digitalis. (Just what we thought.)

Just after New Year's Day about five years later, Madeline came into my office. She asked, "Doctor Jimmie, do you remember me?"

I said, "How could I forget you?" I added, "You look amazing!"

Madeline told me that she had moved back to the Sidney area. It was time for her yearly blood tests, and she asked if I would arrange for her to have the tests and to refill her prescriptions.

Madeline then said, "Guess what?"

As I recall, before I could utter a word she exclaimed, "I'm in love! I have moved back to Sidney to be with my guy."

I thought to myself, "85 years old and happy as a newlywed." I offered her my congratulations and asked in jest, "When can we expect the first newborn?"

She grinned at me and told me, "You are such a kidder, aren't you?" She then said, "If it wasn't for you, I wouldn't be here. I wouldn't have him. I wouldn't be so happy. Thank you!"

I simply said, "You are welcome."

She gave me a hug and a kiss on the cheek.

Madeline then led me into the reception area to meet her guy.

# Winded

In early December of my first year in Sidney I first met Dagne Witman in our hospital emergency room. She was an overweight widow in her mid-sixties who lived in a nearby town north of Sidney. On this day, Dagne complained of being winded.

When I asked Mrs. Witman what she meant by being winded, she replied, "How should I know? You're the doctor!"

When I asked Mrs. Witman if she felt ill right there in the emergency room, she looked me in the eye and stated firmly, "Young man, if I felt good, I wouldn't be here!" Then she said, "I haven't been called Mrs. Witman for forty years. Everyone calls me Dagne or Grandma."

I asked Dagne if she could tell me anymore about how she felt.

She said, "I told you! I'm winded! You know, I can't catch my breath."

I could tell that this interview was going to take a long time.

I remembered my usual sequence of history taking when the discussion bogged down. The sequence included the 5 Ws and H (Who, What, Where, Why, When, and How). Since I already knew the Who (Dagne) and the What (winded), I asked Dagne where she got winded.

She promptly replied, "In my house, where do you think?"

When I asked her what she was doing when she became ill, Dagne said, "Sleeping."

I asked if or when she had any discomfort and she replied, "I have no discomfort. I was winded, just like I said."

I asked, "How often have you been winded?"

Dagne replied, "Every now and then."

"What does that mean?" I asked.

"Off and on for maybe a month. But today it's bad."

All the time Dagne was talking, I noticed that she did not appear to be having any trouble breathing. I asked her if she was winded as we were talking.

"Yes, a little bit. I was a lot worse when I walked in here."

I knew that middle-aged females are notorious for having atypical chest pain. These patients are often misdiagnosed with all sorts of other problems when they have active heart disease. Thinking Dagne may be having some atypical heart pain (angina), I asked her if she ever got winded when she ate.

Dagne replied, "Oh, my, yes. I get bloated real bad with gas. Sometimes those gas pains are whooee! They are bad ones."

"How long have you been having these gas pains?" I countered.

After taking a few moments to think, Dagne stated, "They started on the Fourth of July after I had a hot dog and beans at the town picnic. But they got real bad after Thanksgiving. I hurt all night."

I asked Dagne if she got winded when she had her bad gas pains.

Dagne shot back with, "Wouldn't you be?"

I still thought she might have a cardiac problem. However, I had not excluded other problems that could cause her symptoms, such as problems with her stomach or her gallbladder. I asked Dagne if she had ever been told her gallbladder was bad.

She said, "It's gone. Doctor Reckling took it out years ago."

When I inquired about ever having stomach problems, Dagne said, "Young man, just look at me. Do you think if I had stomach trouble, I could get this fat?"

I didn't respond.

I asked Dagne if the emergency room nurse and I could perform a few tests.

In her own way, Dagne told us to do what we had to do.

I had the laboratory technician obtain some blood for an analysis to be done later, depending upon what I decided after my examination.

The nurse performed an electrocardiogram (ECG) that revealed some nonspecific electrical abnormalities. Upon seeing these anomalies, I asked Dagne to get up and walk a short distance in the emergency room with the ECG electrodes still attached. The ECG with exercise showed changes consistent with acute ischemia (lack of oxygen to the heart tissues).

Dagne also said somewhat matter-of-factly, "I'm getting winded again."

The nurse and I helped Dagne to a bed and had her lie flat. The nurse applied an oxygen mask. Within moments, the abnormal ECG pattern resolved, but Dagne insisted that she was still winded.

I had the nurse place a small nitroglycerin tablet under our patient's tongue. (Nitroglycerin dilates the blood vessels of the heart. This allows for better blood flow to the heart muscle.) Within moments, Dagne said she was no longer winded.

I thought to myself, "We just performed a modified cardiac stress test in the emergency room!"

When she was feeling good again, Dagne wanted to go home. However, I insisted that she stay in the hospital. I told her that I wanted our internal medicine doctor to evaluate her heart.

She consented.

While she was in the hospital, our lab tests excluded an acute heart attack. After his examination, our internist offered Dagne a referral to Billings for an angiogram of her heart (a special x-ray of the blood vessels of the heart) with a possible heart bypass surgery to follow.

She declined. Dagne told us that she was not interested in being cut on by anybody. Afterward, the internist and I persuaded Dagne to take nitroglycerin pills everyday.

I managed Dagne's heart and subsequent health problems for almost twenty years. She died at her home at the age of eighty-five after suffering a stroke.

# Hank

I was already awake early one spring morning when I received a telephone call from my neighbor, Hank. He said, "Doc, did I wake you?"

I replied, "No, Hank. What's on your mind this early in the morning?"

He replied, "I think I might have a little problem. I passed some blood when I went to the bathroom this morning."

Thinking that Hank passed blood when he urinated, I first thought of him passing a kidney stone. I asked if he had any pain.

Being a mild mannered man of few words, Hank said, "No, Doc. No pain."

When I inquired about his having other symptoms such as fever, chills, nausea, burning with urination, vomiting, or cramps, Hank quietly responded, "No, Doc."

As I started to pursue other questions relating to passing bloody urine, Hank interrupted me and said, "Doc, I think you got it all wrong. I don't have any trouble passing my water. I passed blood the other way."

I asked Hank to describe what he passed.

He said, "There was no stool. It was just a big bunch of blood."

I knew that Hank was about eighty-five years old. Also, I knew that bloody stools in a man his age was caused by a colon cancer until proven otherwise. Hoping for a better diagnosis than colon cancer, however, I asked Hank if he ever had any trouble with hemorrhoids.

He said, "No, Doc. Never had any of those."

Hearing this, I told Hank than he really should have his doctor look up inside his rear end to see what's bleeding.

Hank asked, "Doc, do you think it could be serious? I feel so good." After a short pause, he added, "I had one of them colon scopes about five years ago. The doctor told me everything was normal, and I was good for ten years." (Hank thought he could not get a colon cancer for ten years. I did not have the heart to tell him that colonoscopies fail to find cancers about thirty percent of the time.)

To this I suggested to Hank that I still thought he needed to have somebody look inside his bowel. I suggested that he call his doctor's office that morning, tell them that he passed a lot of blood rectally, and he needed to see the doctor soon.

To this suggestion, Hank replied, "I'll do it right after breakfast."

About a month later while mowing my lawn, I noticed Hank in his backyard. He waved to me like he always did. Since he was outside, I assumed he was doing okay.

Hank waited until I had finished my yard work before he telephoned. He asked, "Doc, would you have some time to come over to the house and talk with Martha and me?"

I told Hank I could come right over if that was okay with him.

He replied, "We'd appreciate it."

Martha, Hank's wife, met me at the front door. Always the gracious host, she said, "Jim, it was so nice for you to come right over. Hank isn't feeling too good, you know. We need to talk to you for some advice."

As I entered their front door, I told Martha I would be glad to help any way that I could.

Hank was sitting at their kitchen table sorting some papers. His demeanor seemed about the same, but he appeared pale to me. When Hank stood up to shake my hand, I could see that he had lost some weight. His tall, lanky frame that used to support the muscular, powerfully built body of a hardworking farm boy now seemed frail and vulnerable. Shaking my hand, Hank said, "Thanks for coming over, Doc. I've got some questions for you, if you don't mind."

I told Hank and Martha, "My time is your time."

Hank asked me to sit down.

Martha asked me if she could get me something to drink or perhaps a piece of her bread pudding.

I declined.

Hank said, "Doc, I did just like you told me. I called the clinic, and they got me in to see an urgent care doctor that day. The man's name was Doctor Friday. Doctor Friday put his finger up my behind and sent me over to the G.I. department where one of the fellas set me up for a colon scope. I thought I was gonna die from that stuff they gave me to clean me out before that darn test. Anyway, another doctor scoped me the next morning and told me I had a cancer in my colon. He gave me an appointment to see Doctor Greg Johnson in surgery. Martha and I met with Doctor Johnson. He told us that I needed surgery because the tumor was about to plug me up. A couple days later Doc Johnson took out the cancer. The day after the surgery, another doctor, an oncologist, came to visit me in the hospital. He told us that I needed chemotherapy. The man gave me thirty days to decide, then he left."

I asked Hank what he thought about all this commotion.

Hank said, "Doc, I saw my sister go through chemotherapy. I saw how she suffered. My sister told me that had she been told how bad it was going to be, she never would have done it. I'll tell you Doc, she suffered something awful the rest of her days."

I asked Hank if any of the doctors told him anything about how far advanced his cancer was or how effective the chemotherapy might be.

Hank replied, "I believe Doctor Johnson said he got all of the cancer he could see. The oncologist didn't say much."

I informed Hank that, in my opinion, he did not need chemotherapy. Nobody *needs* chemotherapy. The decision to be treated was his, not his doctor's. I asked Hank what his surgeon thought about his receiving chemotherapy.

Hank said, "Doctor Johnson told me if I was his dad, he would not recommend any more treatment. He thought chemotherapy might give me another week or two, maybe even a month. But I would be sick a lot." Hank paused and said, "Doc, I feel pretty good right now. I don't want to spent the rest of my days in misery."

I told Hank that I agreed with Doctor Johnson. I then offered to find the latest information about chemotherapy and his type of tumor. I told them that I would meet with them later that day.

Using my computer, I researched the latest survival data I could find regarding colon cancer therapy for patients at Hank's age. The literature revealed that Hank's life expectancy was less than a year. Chemotherapy had the potential, though very small, to extend his life *a few days only*. (This is the same data that the oncologists have to give to their patients, if they only would.) Later in the day, I met with Hank and Martha to tell them what I found with my search of the literature.

Before I said a word, Hank told me that he decided not to take chemotherapy right after we talked that morning.

When Hank visited his surgeon for a follow-up visit around Labor Day, he learned from a new CAT scan that there were spots of tumor on his liver, an incurable situation. Doctor Johnson's nurse gave Hank and Martha some literature about the hospice program.

Hank continued to be as active as his condition allowed during the summer and fall months. He tried to keep up with his yard chores, but I saw his exercise tolerance dwindle. My wife Kay and I helped out whenever possible but hopefully not to the point of being intrusive.

During the fall, Hank developed more side effects from his advancing cancer. The oncologist to whom Hank had been assigned by the clinic as his primary doctor refused to see Hank after he declined to take chemotherapy treatments. Hank ended up going back to the urgent care clinic. Despite being referred again several times to the oncology department by doctors in the Urgent Care clinic, Hank was unable to get an appointment with his cancer doctor. Instead, the doctors gave Hank more pills that compounded his symptoms and his misery.

Martha told me, "Nobody will take the time to just sit down with us and give us the facts like you do."

Finally, when Hank's prescription count rose to fifteen or so, Martha asked me to come talk with her husband again. Their daughter had already taken the initiative to stop most of Hank's pills except the ones for pain.

When I saw Hank late in the fall, he appeared quite frail. I knew from experience that his days were numbered. After Hank, Martha, and I had a long talk about everything they had experienced with his cancer care, Martha wanted to know why so many doctors didn't seem to care.

Hank said, "All these doctors say they want me to go to heaven, but none of them want me to die." After a few moments, he muttered, "If they can't take me for my last dime, they don't want to see me." He continued, "Only Doc Johnson and you told us the truth. That is real sad."

I checked in on Hank every few days to see if I could help him in any way.

In November, Hank missed participating in the Veteran's Day parade, something he had done every year since coming home from World War II as a decorated veteran.

In early January, Hank and Martha contacted the local Hospice program for assistance. However, they asked me to explain just about everything the hospice workers did and the medicines they prescribed. Hank, and especially Martha, had become distrustful of all their caregivers and their medicines, a sad thing indeed.

Later in January, I visited Hank on a day when he was having uncontrollable abdominal pain. As I was helping Hank in the bathroom, he told me, "I saw too many men die in the Pacific. I am not afraid to die when my time comes. I know I'm getting close."

I leaned over and spoke into Hank's ear. I said, "Hank, I think so too." Thereafter, I asked Martha to give Hank pain medicine often to "keep him comfortable."

Martha telephoned me about 6 o'clock the next morning. She said, "Jim, would you come over. I think I just lost my Hank?"

Promptly, I grabbed my bag and walked through the snow to their home next door. Hank was lying face up in his bed with Martha holding his hand. His face was pale and his eyes were closed. Placing my stethoscope on Hank's chest, I heard no heart tones or breath sounds. Hank was already cold to my touch. I could not feel a pulse. I looked at Martha and said, "Martha, Hank's gone. He won't have pain anymore." Then, I gave her a hug.

At Hank's funeral and near his obituary in the newspaper, Martha placed a "Thank-you" note to Doctor Johnson and me. Martha had nothing kind to say about how others in the health care team treated her Hank, so she said nothing. That was Hank's way.

Hank was buried with full military honors on a cold January day in Montana.

# Natural Wonders

"Women are like teabags; you never know how strong
they are until they're put in hot water."

Eleanor Roosevelt

# By the Book

Caroline, accompanied by her husband Robert, came to the hospital in labor one summer afternoon. Caroline had neither sought out nor received any prenatal care. The pair had verified the pregnancy with an over-the-counter pregnancy kit. Afterward, they ventured to the local library for a book on how to have a baby. Against the advice of their respective relatives, they shunned any medical advice during the pregnancy because having a baby was just natural.

I was summoned to see Caroline because I was on OB call for the weekend. When I entered the hospital room, I noticed that Robert was reading a book titled "Prepared Childbirth Without Pain." After I introduced myself to the couple, I asked Caroline if she knew her estimated due date.

She told me that it was two weeks from this day.

I asked if someone had given her a specific date for her delivery.

She replied that they had figured out the date using the book.

About this time, Caroline started to have a contraction. Robert stated, "The book says that you need to take long, slow breaths during the contractions and finish with a cleansing breath." Caroline responded with the requested breathing technique for the duration of the contraction.

I asked Caroline if she recalled her last normal menstrual cycle. When she gave me a date that she had written down in a diary, I determined that her pregnancy was about thirty-eight weeks along. My examination confirmed the dates of the pregnancy. I deduced that Caroline was indeed near term and in labor.

Robert wanted to know how many centimeters his wife was dilated.

I told the pair that I would need to perform a vaginal examination to determine that measurement.

Robert blurted out, "Well do it! I can't tell her how to breathe unless I know how many centimeters her cervix is open."

My examination revealed the cervix to be only two centimeters dilated. I knew from experience that Caroline had a long way to go before she gave birth because this was her first pregnancy.

Caroline and Robert were prepared with their notepads, pencils, recording graphs, and the book.

After several hours, my curiosity got the best of me. I just had to ask about the book.

Robert told me that they had received it at a prepared childbirth class just a few days before. They knew that they had plenty of time to learn the book before Caroline went into labor because she was more than two weeks before her due date.

I asked the couple if they understood that the EDC, or the estimated date of confinement, was just that, an estimate. A full term pregnancy was anytime between 38 to 42 weeks after conception.

They agreed that they had made a small error with the date but felt that things were going well so far.

Caroline's labor was intense and progressed slowly. By the middle of the night, Caroline still refused any medication for discomfort. Robert continued to give breathing instructions from the book. Robert started performing total body massages to decrease Caroline's muscle cramping and backaches.

Just before breakfast, after sixteen hours of vigorous labor, Caroline was ready to give birth. The nurses escorted the pair to the delivery room in a manner similar to that prescribed in the book. While Caroline was lying on the delivery room table, her contractions became even more intense, a normal phenomenon as the baby's head moves farther down in the birth canal. Unfortunately, Robert had not read this chapter. His only exhortation to Caroline with each contraction was, "Breathe faster!"

Soon Caroline was working extremely hard as the baby's head reached the pelvic outlet. Her face was covered with sweat. Her gown was soaking wet. It took all of her concentration to remain in control over her labor pains and to keep her psyche intact. Unfortunately, with so much rapid breathing, Caroline developed severe leg cramps that put her over the mental edge.

As her husband continued dutifully to bark out instructions, Caroline reached her mental limit. She shouted to her husband, "Shut up! Throw away that dang book! It's not working anymore! I'm in pain!"

Her husband appeared stunned. He too was exhausted.

Caroline started to push continuously to get her baby out. She yelled, "Doctor Ashcraft, Get that baby out of me NOW! I want some morphine NOW!"

It was too late in the delivery process to give morphine. Therefore, I applied a suction cup appearing apparatus (a vacuum extractor) to the baby's head. A small amount of traction by me coupled with a single hard push from Caroline delivered the baby.

I exclaimed to the couple, "It's a boy!"

The baby cried vigorously when I wiped his face, but the mom was too exhausted to notice. Robert placed his head on the table next to Caroline and closed his eyes. He too was exhausted.

I had the nurse care for the baby while I waited for the delivery of the afterbirth. When everything was done on my end of the table, the nurse placed the baby next to Caroline's face. Barely able to stay awake, Caroline looked at her baby and said, "I did it."

Several years later, Robert and Caroline brought a newborn baby girl to my office for a checkup and a birth certificate. Caroline and Robert finished reading the book and delivered a baby at home.

It was *just natural* and by the book.

# It's Personal

I met Sheila for the first time when she came to the office for her initial obstetrics visit. She was twenty-eight years old, and this was her first pregnancy. Sheila was absolutely giddy with excitement because she thought that she would never be able to conceive a child. Apparently, a gynecology specialist told her she had a tipped uterus that caused her fertility problems (all uteri are tipped in some direction).

Near the end of our first visit, Sheila asked if it would be okay with me if her husband accompanied her on future visits. I assured her that her husband would be most welcome in my office.

Sheila's next OB visit was about a month later. She remained as excited as I had remembered. Her husband Jason was just as enthusiastic. The pair had gone from near depression for their want of a child to near ecstasy with this pregnancy. When I examined Sheila's abdomen and listened to the fetus, Jason wanted to assist. I had no problem with this activity since it seemed to give the pair such joy.

I learned that Jason had been a combat medic in Vietnam for a year. He had been involved in multiple battles, had tended to many wounded, and had received a Silver Star for valor in combat. I was more than willing to allow him to measure his wife's abdomen and to listen to his baby's heartbeat if he would recount some of his war experiences.

As the pregnancy progressed, Sheila and Jason made every appointment. At each visit, I allowed Jason the opportunity to measure his wife's abdomen and to listen to his baby's heart tones. The pair started prepared childbirth classes when Sheila was twenty-four weeks pregnant. I attempted to answer their lists of questions at each clinic visit.

Sheila went into labor near her due date. After the nurses settled Sheila into a hospital bed, Jason continued to ask questions of the nurses and me about the events going on around them. Jason was a magnificent coach for a prepared childbirth. He did not leave his wife's bedside during the entire labor.

Sheila was moved to the delivery suite when she felt like pushing. Of course, Jason came along. He was not going to miss this for anything. He and Sheila were well prepared for this event.

Sheila pushed like a real trooper with each contraction. She even smiled and joked after each contraction because she knew that she was closer to something she was not supposed to have, a baby. Jason was as excited as his wife. When the baby's head was crowning (appearing at the pelvic outlet), Jason asked permission to touch the baby's head.

I encouraged him to do so.

As the baby's head emerged from the mom, I asked Sheila not to push so I could suck out the baby's mouth and nose. I turned to ask Jason if he wanted to deliver his newborn baby, but he wasn't in his chair beside Sheila. I stood up briefly and saw Jason in a neutral corner of the delivery room slipping to the floor. He had passed out!

I asked the nurse to watch the dad while Sheila finished her work.

A baby girl came out just fine and screaming to the delight of her mom. Sheila was so excited I thought she was going to jump off the delivery table to take her baby from me. After I cleaned and dried the newborn, I placed her next to Sheila's face. The nurse covered them with a blanket.

While I continued with the delivery of the afterbirth and sutured a small tear on Sheila's bottom, I had the nurse check on the new dad. Jason remained asleep against the wall. He had missed the grand finale.

I thought to myself, "I never had a dad as prepared for a birth as this one. A war medic who had seen trauma far greater than the birth of a baby....what gives?" Then I thought, "In war, he could isolate himself emotionally. Here it was personal, very personal."

The nurse applied a cold washcloth to Jason's face to arouse him. He had missed only a few moments of the process, *the most important moments*! However, all was good when he saw his wife aglow with pride and his perfect new baby daughter.

Sheila asked, "Doctor Ashcraft, would it be okay with you if we named her Ashlee after you?"

I replied, "I would be honored."

# Attack

Cynthia was a quiet, diminutive cowgirl who at age twenty-three was pregnant with her first child. Cynthia always insisted on having appointments in the midmorning so she would have plenty of time to drive into town from their ranch. When she came to the clinic for her prenatal visits, her husband Nathan always accompanied her. Since Cynthia was a very modest woman, Nathan remained in the reception area while my nurse and I examined his wife. After her OB examination, Cynthia and Nathan always had a date lunch in town before going home.

This pattern was consistent until Cynthia was about eight months pregnant. My nurse came into my office early one morning to ask if I could see Cynthia and Nathan before clinic hours started. My nurse told me that Cynthia was crying and it looked like Nathan had been in an accident. I stopped whatever I was doing and asked my nurse to bring them back into the examination area.

Standing in the hallway outside my office, I watched Cynthia and Nathan walk down the hallway toward the examination area. I thought to myself, "Aren't they a sight?" Cynthia was about five-feet two-inches tall with a big, bulging belly. Nathan was about six-feet two-inches tall and muscular. From behind, I could see that they both walked with a waddle, Cynthia because of her pregnancy and Nathan because of his bowlegs. The nurse escorted them into an examination room.

When I entered the room, Cynthia was still crying. Nathan had a bloody nose, a black eye, and a red, puffy face. I asked the pair what happened to them.

Cynthia cried out, "Doctor Ashcraft, I tried to kill my husband!" After a few sobs, she looked at Nathan and said, "Honey, I am so sorry."

At best I was bewildered. I asked Cynthia what she had done exactly.

She cried, "I tried to kill my husband and I don't even remember!"

I looked at Nathan who looked really beat up. I asked him if he could tell me what happened.

Nathan started, "Well Doc, I was sound asleep this morning when all of a sudden I felt a slap on my face. When I woke up I couldn't move. Cynthia had pinned down my shoulders with her legs, and she was sitting smack dab on top of my chest. I asked her what the heck she was doing. She didn't answer me. She just slugged me in the nose."

Still crying, Cynthia moaned, "Honey, I didn't mean it."

Nathan continued, "Doc, then she started babbling something like 'You're not going to rape me and hurt my baby,' and started in beating on my face again." After a short pause to think, Nathan continued, "I tried to talk to her, but she just wouldn't listen. I think she was dreaming."

I asked what happened next.

Nathan told me that after an unknown amount of time Cynthia woke up with her hand raised ready to hit him again. She wanted to know what was going on. When Cynthia looked at his face she started to cry.

Cynthia asked, "Doctor Ashcraft, am I crazy?"

Looking at the pair I could barely keep from laughing. This little pregnant woman had given her two-hundred-pound cowboy quite a thrashing, and she didn't remember doing it! I suggested to them that, most likely, Cynthia was acting out a dream. Unfortunately for Nathan her acting out was very real.

I examined Nathan and found that his nose was broken but still straight. He had bruises, abrasions, and contusions only on his face that I figured would be healed by the time Cynthia delivered their baby.

Cynthia had abrasions on her knuckles and some dried blood on her fingers. Her eyes were red and puffy from crying. More important, however, was that her baby was doing just fine.

When Nathan heard his baby's heart sounds for the first time a big smile came over his face. He gave Cynthia a hug and told her everything was okay now.

Afterward, Nathan became more involved with Cynthia's care. He accompanied Cynthia for her remaining OB examinations. A month or so later he sat next to his wife in the hospital room during labor. After Cynthia delivered a healthy baby boy, Nathan cut the umbilical cord.

As the years passed I had the opportunity to assist Cynthia with two more pregnancies that produced healthy children.

As far as I know, Nathan received no more beatings in the middle of night.

# That's How It's Done

At age twenty-two, Dana Verden delivered a healthy baby boy. He was born about a month before Dana's expected due date after she labored for only six hours (the usual first time labor is about sixteen hours). Dana told me later that he just blasted out.

Dana's second pregnancy occurred about two years later. This time she was carrying twins. Unfortunately, there were some complications at twenty-four weeks into the pregnancy. Her obstetrician in another community advised Dana and her husband that the best chance of trying to save her very premature babies was a Cesarean section (an abdominal operation to remove the babies). (The doctors did not tell Dana and her husband that the chances of her very premature babies surviving at all with the operation were about 100,000 to 1. Nor did the doctors tell the couple that, if their children survived, the chance of their being permanently damaged was almost 100 percent.) Dana had the operation. Her twins weighed less than two pounds each and died soon after birth.

Several years later, I was called to the emergency room to attend a woman in labor. The emergency room nurse advised me that the woman got mad at her obstetrician in a nearby hospital and left. Apparently, she went into labor while traveling home and ended up at the Sidney hospital. The nurse told me that the woman had had a previous Cesarean section, and her uterine cervix was already eight centimeters dilated (ten centimeters is full dilatation). The baby was coming out headfirst.

I rushed to the hospital from my home four miles north of town. While I was in transit, the nurse moved the woman to the delivery room. When I arrived a few minutes later, the woman's cervix was ten centimeters dilated. I first met Dana when she was lying on the delivery room table ready to have a baby.

Dana told me that she had no problems with delivering her first baby. After her Cesarean section, she was advised to see an obstetrician to have a VBAC delivery (vaginal birth after C-section), which she did. Dana told me that she had discussed a VBAC delivery with the obstetrician her entire pregnancy. The obstetrician, supposedly, was agreeable to this arrangement. However, after she checked into the hospital, the obstetrician waited until Dana had just a couple weak uterine contractions,

told her that she couldn't deliver vaginally, and started to prepare her for another operation.

Dana told me that her obstetrician made her really mad. She
put on her clothes and headed home to the shock of the staff at
the hospital. Dana went into labor about ten miles outside of Sidney, so her husband just drove to our emergency room. She said,
"Doctors think they know everything about having babies."

Quickly, I advised Dana of the potential risks of delivering a
baby after a previous Cesarean section, including rupturing her
uterus through the old scar (statistically, the uterine rupture
rate is only about one percent or less).

After she agreed that I had told her the VBAC potential complication facts, in brief, Dana pushed for just a few minutes
before she delivered a healthy boy infant at term weighing
almost nine pounds. The remainder of the delivery process was
uneventful. I checked the uterus carefully for lacerations and
found none. Dana remained in her birthing bed while I took her
child to the newborn nursery for an evaluation. Her total time in
labor was about three hours.

Afterward, Dana pronounced, "Doc, now that's how it's supposed to be done!"

I had to agree. Dana had done a good job. She now had two
boys.

Dana allowed the nursing staff at the hospital and me to
watch her and her newborn son for another day in the hospital
before she insisted on going home.

About a year later, Dana was again pregnant. Her prenatal
course was totally unremarkable. Again, we discussed the rules
for VBAC delivery.

Near her due date, Dana labored about an hour to deliver a
healthy female child weighing more than eight pounds. Again,
there were no complications during the delivery process. This
time, the Verden family had the girl they had cherished. Since
she had delivered later in the day, Dana agreed to stay in the
hospital overnight. She left the hospital before noon the next day.

Two years later, Dana returned pregnant. Once more, we discussed the rules for VBAC delivery. Again, her prenatal course
was unremarkable. Again, there were no complications during
the delivery process. This time, Dana labored for only about
thirty minutes to deliver a healthy female infant. She delivered
this baby before breakfast and went home by suppertime.

A year or so passed before Dana came to the office bearing another child. This time, I breezed past the VBAC discussion because she almost knew it by heart. Again, her prenatal course was unremarkable. Near her due day, Dana entered our hospital in labor and soon delivered a healthy male infant. She wanted to leave the hospital right away, but after a discussion about getting some quality rest, which she had not been getting with her three other toddlers at home, Dana agreed to stay overnight. Amazingly, she stayed two extra nights.

Before leaving the hospital, Dana related that she thought she had this baby thing figured out. She hinted that she might just stay home the next time.

I just smiled.

# Mother Knows Best

His Texas-based employer transferred Scott Helford to Sidney during the oil boom in the 1970s. Scott came with his wife Barbara and their two young children.

I met Barbara a few months after their arrival for a possible prenatal visit. If pregnant, this would be her fourth. Barbara, now about thirty years old, told me she had a miscarriage the previous year when she was about three months pregnant. Since that time, Barbara related that her cycles were normal. Now she had missed a menstrual cycle and felt pregnant.

My nurse performed a pregnancy test on Barbara's urine. Her pregnancy was confirmed.

After a discussion about the obstetrical care my clinic staff and I provided and after receiving our usual packet of prenatal literature, Barbara agreed to have her first examination in a month. She made her next appointment before leaving the clinic.

My first examination of Barbara occurred when she was about twelve weeks pregnant. Except for some morning sickness and breast engorgement, Barbara's examination was unremarkable. Her uterus was about twelve weeks in size and matched her menstrual dates. It was too early to detect fetal heart tones. (Electronic dopplers were not widely used in obstetrics at this time. Today, heart tones can be detected easily with electronic monitors around ten weeks of gestation.)

At sixteen weeks gestation, Barbara returned for another prenatal visit. This time, she brought her husband, Scott, to hear the baby's heart tones. After completing my prenatal evaluation, we all listened to the new baby's heart sounds. Both parents seemed to be truly excited about this pregnancy. After I had answered all their questions, Barbara scheduled another appointment for the next month.

At her twenty-week evaluation, Barbara told me that both her breasts became very engorged and tender that morning. She did not recall being bumped by her children when they were playing. Otherwise, Barbara related that she felt fine.

My examination revealed Barbara's uterus to be at a twenty-week size. Her weight and vital signs remained good. When she heard the baby's heart tones again, Barbara smiled.

My examination of Barbara's breasts, however, was not normal. Instead of having normal engorgement from her pregnancy, Barbara's breasts were almost rock-hard, hot, and very tender to minimal external pressure. A bloody discharge oozed from the nipples. I knew Barbara had something abnormal happening with her breasts that potentially was very bad.

I told Barbara that I didn't know what she had and that I would call a specialist for a consultation. I went to my office and telephoned the University of Washington Medical School. When I talked to the obstetrician on call and gave him my patient's history, the doctor noted that it sounded as if my patient had an acute inflammatory breast cancer. He thought that my patient should have a biopsy soon and offered to accept Barbara as a patient, if she wished.

After this, I returned to see Barbara. I related to her that the specialist thought she should have a biopsy of her breast soon. I did not say a word about cancer.

Barbara looked at me and said, "It's bad, isn't it? I can feel it."

I told her I did not know what was wrong with her breasts. However, because she was pregnant, I told her that I would like to perform a breast biopsy using a local anesthetic. (At the time in Sidney, all breast biopsies were done at our hospital using a general anesthetic.)

She agreed.

The next morning, using only a local anesthetic, I performed a small breast biopsy in each breast in our clinic's minor surgery room. I sent the tissue samples to the pathologist and told Barbara that I would telephone the results when I received them. In the meantime, I prescribed some narcotic pain pills for her discomfort.

The pathologist called me later that day and told me that his preliminary frozen sections of the breast tissue looked bad. He said it looked like a cancer, but he couldn't give me a final report until his stained tissue slides were done in a couple of days.

The final report returned as *anaplastic inflammatory breast cancer,* the most aggressive kind of tumor. I consulted an oncologist in Billings before I talked with Barbara and her husband. The oncologist wanted to see my patient and her husband the next day and gave me a tentative appointment for them.

I asked Barbara and her husband to come into the clinic that day for a discussion. We met at the end of my clinic hours that afternoon. When I gave the couple Barbara's bad diagnosis, they both cried. Again, Barbara told me that she knew it was something bad. They agreed to visit with the oncologist the next day in Billings.

The oncologist telephoned me several days later. He informed me that Barbara's tumor was highly hormone sensitive, and her pregnancy was making it grow out of control. He also said that he told Barbara and her husband that her only chance of survival, which was slim at best, was to have an abortion. The doctor told me that Barbara declined his offer.

When I asked about any next course of treatment, the oncologist replied, "Let's hope she's able to have a good baby." The oncologist offered me his further assistance in managing Barbara's case. Additionally, he gave me the names of Ob-Gyn cancer specialists at the University of Washington Medical School and the University of Colorado Medical School.

Barbara, Scott, and I visited when they returned to Sidney. They gave me their version of their visit with the Billings oncologist. The two stories were amazingly similar. The couple declined an abortion. Any chemotherapy or radiation that might be used to treat the tumor was considered toxic to the baby, so Barbara declined treatment. Besides, the oncologist estimated Barbra's chances of survival in months, not years. Barbara just hoped that she would last long enough to have a healthy baby.

Knowing the complications created by the breast cancer, the Helfords wanted to know if I was willing to continue providing Barbara's OB care or if they should find another doctor out of town.

I agreed to continue caring for Barbara.

Barbara had a difficult time with pain during the last half of her pregnancy. However, I remember that she always smiled whenever she heard her baby's heart tones. Barbara went into labor near her due date and delivered a healthy baby boy.

Because of the cancer, Barbara was unable to breast feed her newborn. This distressed her considerably.

Soon after their son's birth, the Helfords moved back to Texas to be near their families.

Scott sent me a note months later. Barbara died when her son was six months old.

# Giving Back

We make a living by what we get, we make a life by what we give.

Sir Winston Churchill

# Let's Play Ball

By getting involved in a few community projects, I learned some things about getting a project completed with volunteer help. First, most people will gladly volunteer their time for just about anything. Second, despite their best intentions, most volunteers never show up as promised or work as long as they promised. Third, people do not want to volunteer their money. Fourth, most people are more than willing to donate their stuff or their time on short notice for a small project than to commit to an extensive project sometime in the future.

My wife Kay and I always loved to play baseball or softball. Since our first two children were girls, softball became their summertime sport.

Despite laws for equal opportunity for boys and girls, the city of Sidney was a bit behind the curve when it came to equal opportunities in sports. The boys had a ball field for Legion baseball, one for Babe Ruth baseball, and five for Little League Baseball. The girls were allowed to use two of the oldest Little League fields for their games. The boys' fields were maintained well by the city of Sidney and the local baseball commission. The girls' fields seemed to be maintained as an afterthought. Much of the maintenance was performed by parents and by the girls playing softball.

On a Thursday afternoon (my day out of the office) a short time before the softball season started, Kay and I were cleaning up the girls' ball fields when we noticed how hard the dirt infield was. I thought all the dirt areas could use a good loosening with a rototiller. (I just happened to have a PTO-driven tiller on the back of my John Deere garden tractor that weighed three hundred pounds that I thought could do the job.) After a short discussion about what needed to be fixed, Kay and I ventured to the city hall to speak with the manager of the Parks and Recreation Department. We spoke with the manager of the Public Works Department who gave us permission to work on the fields with the admonition, *"As long as you don't mess things up."*

The next Saturday morning, Kay and I arrived early with our children to start our project. While Kay and the children picked up debris around the fence line, I drove my tractor with the tiller attached onto the ball field. My first attempt at tilling was unsuccessful because the tiller tines could not penetrate the hard infield surface. I asked Kay to stand on the tiller to add more weight. The tiller still could not penetrate the hard surface.

I then had a grand idea to use a plow to break up the soil. I figured I could use my tiller afterward to smooth the dirt. While Kay and the kids continued with their tasks, I drove to the local John Deere dealership to find a tractor with a plow. I met with the owner of the business and asked him if I could rent one of his farm tractors with a plow for a couple hours.

He wanted to know why.

After I explained my dilemma with the hard soil on the softball fields, he asked about how long I would need the tractor because his shop closed at noon.

I told him I hoped to be done in an hour.

The owner raised his hand and asked me to wait a minute. He went to the front door of his business and looked around his acres of tools and tractors. When he returned the owner told me, "Take that 3040 out there with the three-bottom" (3040 is a ninety-horsepower tractor; three-bottom is a type of plow with three cutting blades).

I asked him, "What's the charge?"

He thought for a moment and asked, "It's for the girls you say?"

When I nodded yes, he instructed me to use the tractor for as long as I needed it and to be sure to park it in the same spot when I was finished.

I walked to the tractor and climbed inside. It was larger than the fifty-horsepower John Deere I had at home but the controls were similar. I felt right at home driving the mile or so to the softball fields.

When I arrived at the ball fields, I drove onto Field #2 to get started. I lowered the plow onto the dirt infield, increased the tractor's throttle a little for more power, and let out the clutch in second gear so I wouldn't go too fast. The plow engaged, and the tractor rolled about twenty feet before it stopped. I had hit a really hard spot already, so I thought.

I increased the power some and nothing happened.

When I pushed the throttle to full power the front tractor wheels raised up, and the tractor lurched forward another ten feet or so. Looking backward, I saw the plow sitting on top of a large piece of concrete. I wondered what I had done now.

Kay and I inspected the ground that I had just damaged. We found more concrete, rocks, steel bars, and other kinds of junk. I reminded myself of the words of the Public Works director, *"as long as you don't mess things up."* I thought to myself, "Boy, now look what you've done."

Kay and I decided that I should finish plowing up the infield since I had already made a mess of the ground. With all the debris so close to the infield surface we did not feel that the area was safe for our kids to play ball much less other parents' kids.

The tractor and plow slowly ripped up the infields with little difficulty. The job, however, took almost three hours to complete and not the one hour that I estimated. I got the tractor back to the John Deere dealership about three o'clock that Saturday afternoon.

On Monday, Kay and I went to talk with the Public Works director about what we uncovered under the ball fields. While we were waiting for him to arrive, we discussed our adventure with one of the mayor's secretaries. She told us that she was not surprised at our discoveries under the infield surface. She informed us that the ball fields were built upon an old dumpsite for military housing that had been demolished after World War II. Apparently, the junk had gradually made its way to the surface over the years.

I thought to myself, "Now they tell us!"

After Kay and I reassured the Public Works director that we would make the fields ready in time for the beginning of the softball season, he told us that the city would be available to haul away the debris that we unearthed.

That afternoon, I happened to meet the owner of the Sidney Red-E-Mix Company. During a casual conversation, I mentioned my ball field dilemma to him. Without hesitation he told me about his gravel rock sorter that he could bring to the ball fields. He said the thing would remove anything bigger than a pea.

I asked him what it would cost.

He said, "I have girls too, remember?" He then said, "Doc, go worry about something more important than dirt."

Within a few days, a crew from the Sidney Red-E-Mix had removed several dump trucks full of debris from the infields and brought in enough good dirt to level out the playing surfaces.

All Kay and I had to do now was to replace the lines and bases on the field. On Thursday afternoon Kay and I were back at the ball fields to smooth out the infield dirt using my garden tractor pulling a small land leveler and to replace the home plate and the bases. Unfortunately, we discovered the original field boundaries and measurements were not correct by a large margin. The angle at home plate is supposed to be ninety degrees. The angle we discovered was only seventy degrees. In addition, the infield was not square. Each base path was a different length. I knew that Kay and I could measure the field correctly, but it was going to take more time than we had that day.

It was getting dark as Kay and I were planning how we could find time to get the fields measured and in playing condition. We were getting ready to leave for the day when Bart Mason and his survey crew from Interstate Engineering arrived. They were on their way home from work and stopped to see what we were doing in the dark.

After I explained our dilemma, I asked Bart if he needed a small job.

He replied, "Not really, what's on your mind?"

I replied, "Measuring ball fields. What would it cost me?"

His foreman interjected, "Hey, man, not now. I'm tired."

Bart looked at his men and asked, "Maybe Saturday morning on our way out of town?"

The foreman nodded his head in agreement. He thought their team could have the job done quickly.

Again, I asked, "What's this going to cost me?"

One of the workers replied, "How about a six pack of beer and pizza after work?"

I replied, "One for each of you?"

The fellow said, "No, one six pack for all of us. We're trying to cut down. Ha!"

When Kay and I arrived at the ballpark Saturday morning, the survey crew was already finishing their job. The foreman told us, "This field was really crooked but not any more. We put survey stakes deep in the ground for home plate, the bases, and the outfield fence lines. You are all set to go!"

After I thanked them I asked, "When do you want your beer and pizza?"

Bart said, "Can't drink now. We're working. We'll let you know, okay?"

I agreed. (Bart never called me for the beer and pizza.)

Our family resumed the cleanup project. By now, some other parents had arrived to help. Together, our community team added new roofs to the dugouts, cleaned out the restrooms, and readied the concession building. The softball season started in only a week or so.

One of the volunteers was acquainted with the management of the Blue Rock Beverage Company, the local Pepsi-Cola bottling company. She suggested that we ask Blue Rock if they would be interested in replacing the field's old, tattered scoreboard.

I thought her idea was a good one. Unfortunately, I forgot to make the inquiry.

Someone else, however, made the inquiry. Before the girls' softball season opener, the new, improved, squared, and measured softball fields sported new scoreboards with the Pepsi-Cola logo.

Sitting on the bleachers that first game, I truly enjoyed it when the home plate umpire shouted, "**Ladies, let's play ball!**"

# Good Teacher, Bad Teacher

One afternoon a female resident physician approached me in the outpatient clinic and said, "Doctor Ashcraft, I have a problem with Doctor Jellison, my surgery preceptor. Can I talk with you about it?"

I could see that the young physician was upset. We found a quiet area nearby where we could speak freely.

When I asked her to tell me more about her problem, she said, "This surgeon is really a jerk. He treats me as if I don't exist. He throws instruments in surgery. He yells at the nurses and treats them like dirt. He doesn't talk with his patients and leaves me to answer their questions, which I can't do. He doesn't let me do anything in surgery. I really hate him! What should I do?"

I replied to the young doctor, "It sounds to me like this guy is a really good teacher."

The resident looked stunned. She glared at me and exclaimed, "Doctor Ashcraft, what have you been smoking? Are you nuts? This guy is not a good teacher! In fact, he may be the worst teacher I have ever had! He is just an unprofessional jerk!"

Sensing her frustration, I replied, "If we agree that a student learns a lot from a good teacher and you have learned a lot about what not to do from this doctor, then I would say he indeed is a good teacher. He has taught you how not to care for your patients and how not to treat nurses."

After a few moments of thought, she responded with, "Well, maybe."

I advised the resident that I would contact the surgeon and see what could be done with her situation.

Having had a similar experience with one of my surgery preceptors as an intern, I vaguely knew how to approach this doctor. Instead of a direct confrontation, I elected to send the doctor a thank-you card. I obtained a blank generic card from the residency secretary and composed this message:

Dear Doctor Jellison,

Thank you for your efforts to help educate our residents.
Your time and expertise are appreciated by our faculty and staff.

Best wishes,
Jimmie Ashcraft, M.D.

I mailed the card that afternoon.

Several weeks later, the young resident physician approached me while I was making rounds in the hospital. She reminded me of our conversation regarding her difficulties with her surgeon preceptor and then asked, "Doctor Ashcraft, what did you say to Doctor Jellison?"

I asked what was wrong now.

She responded, "Nothing. Absolutely nothing. He has been so nice the past few weeks. He's taking time to explain things. He lets me close wounds in surgery. He's even nicer to the floor nurses and the scrub techs. What did you say to him?"

I told the young doctor that I said nothing to Doctor Jellison.

She asked, "Then what did you do? He's so different."

I informed the resident of my positive thank-you note. I told her, "Perhaps Doctor Jellison thought that if we appreciated his teaching efforts when he wasn't trying, then maybe he could be a really good teacher if he put forth some effort. By your comments, it appears that my guess paid off."

The resident said, "I have learned a lot from Doctor Jellison, both good and bad. I guess you were right. He is a good teacher!"

The surgeon continued to provide good teaching experiences for our residents.

# Epilogue

We'll have to learn to get along with one another. We'll have to be more aware of responsibilities which go with this rapidly speeding up world. We'll have to set examples for those who will follow us and recognize that we don't know it all. So we should listen to the other person, and that other person sometimes is right and sometimes we are wrong. It will be a matter of accommodation and compromise, knowledge and understanding.

Mike Mansfield 1989
Montana Senator
Ambassador to Japan

# Art versus Science

When I was a boy, Mickey Mantle and Doctor P.E. Wally were my heroes. Doctor Wally came to our home when my brothers and I were sick or injured, and he always made us better. I sensed that he always knew what to do to help us. As I grew up and suffered more illnesses and injuries, I had absolute faith in my doctors. I admired them all. Why wouldn't I? No matter what happened to me, I always recovered after they cared for me. I knew that doctors had to be the smartest people around. I wanted to be like them. I wanted to help people.

As I worked my way toward medical school and learned how to think like a scientist, I became convinced that medicine was an orderly, scientific field of knowledge. From my small sphere of experience and limited understanding, I perceived that my doctors always were able to figure out difficult diagnostic problems by using logical, scientific reasoning.

Early in medical school, I learned a lot about human anatomy and physiology along with the techniques to examine the human body. I was taught to treat my patients after performing a thorough history and physical examination and after correlating my findings with the scientific information known at the time to make the correct diagnosis. I remember one preceptor telling me, "There is nothing more important than the goddamn diagnosis."

With the correct diagnosis made, the appropriate treatment was supposed to be obvious. The implication from the teachings of many medical school professors was that there was *always* a correct diagnosis that should be followed by an appropriate treatment. As a young medical student, I had not yet begun to comprehend a physician's limitations in both scientific knowledge and human skills when making the correct diagnosis. Only after I started my clinical rotations did I start to appreciate the dilemmas, the uncertainties, and the imprecision that compounded the making of the correct diagnosis. I garnered firsthand experience with medicine's all-to-common *adverse events*.

While discussing the care of the sick child, one of my pediatric professors was trying to explain how well the human body responds to keep itself well. I recall that he told our medical school class, "Five percent of sick children will die no matter what we do for them. Ninety-five percent will survive, no matter what doctors and parents do to them. Often we don't know what to do, either way."

During my internship when I had to apply the science of my medical school training, I learned to appreciate how doctors had treated me in the past was often determined not by scientific medical facts but by their gut feelings, their intuition, their experience, or their best guesses.

After I went into private practice and my experience accumulated, I was amazed at how often the traumatized human body could mend without my help if given enough time. At other times, I learned that my best efforts to save patients with severe trauma became futile exercises in physiology and pharmacology.

I've held the hands of elderly patients who, after losing a loved one, forfeited their will to live and died from broken hearts. I've held the hands of mothers with broken hearts who had lost a child and wanted to die but couldn't because their other children needed love too.

I had the good fortune of assisting over seventeen hundred babies into this world. I learned that few experiences can match the euphoria of a healthy baby's first cries or that none can match the profound sadness when a baby dies.

As an educator, I had the opportunity to share my clinical experiences with and convey what I knew to community members, high school students, medical students, nurses, volunteer emergency personnel, and physicians-in-training. I am sure I learned as much or more from them as they learned from me.

Some catchwords of today include "quality care" and "evidence-based medicine." Unfortunately, nobody can define quality care. The idea of quality in healthcare is in the mind of the beneficiary of the care. We know that evidence-based care explains, at best, twenty percent or less of what health care providers actually do to their patients. The remaining eighty percent of healthcare falls into the category that includes gut feelings, intuition, experience, or best guesses. This later category is what makes medicine an art and not a pure science.

Despite how the various media promote spectacular medical advances and healthcare successes, medicine remains a business of people caring for people. The media would make us believe that healthcare is an orderly and scientific activity. It is not. It is an endeavor of fallible doctors caring for patients who are equally fallible. The clinician is armed with an incomplete science base, a constantly changing knowledge base, and information that is often unreliable. There is a major gulf between what doctors really know and what they do.

Despite how medicine has become intertwined in our daily lives with the media, what really happens in healthcare remains mostly hidden from the public's eye. The capabilities of the *science* of medicine are frequently misunderstood, misrepresented, or overstated by the media, healthcare professionals, and advertisers. The populace, including physicians and other healthcare providers, presume the *science* of medicine to be more perfect than it is.

Unfortunately, these same people all too often fail to comprehend and appreciate how astonishing and fulfilling the *art* of medicine is and can be.

The stories in this book, along with those in my first book, *Reflections of a Country Doctor*, give a snapshot of my experiences becoming a doctor and serving people as a family doc in the trenches of rural America.

I believe my wife Kay and I had a positive influence in our rural Montana community. When all is said and done, I guess making a positive difference in other peoples' lives is all anyone could ever expect.

CPSIA information can be obtained at www.ICGtesting.com
Printed in the USA
LVOW091914280911

248337LV00001B/8/P